GUIDE TO COAST GUARD CUTTERS & SMALL BOATS

Coast Guard vessels in service
between 18 feet and 420 feet

1970 -2024

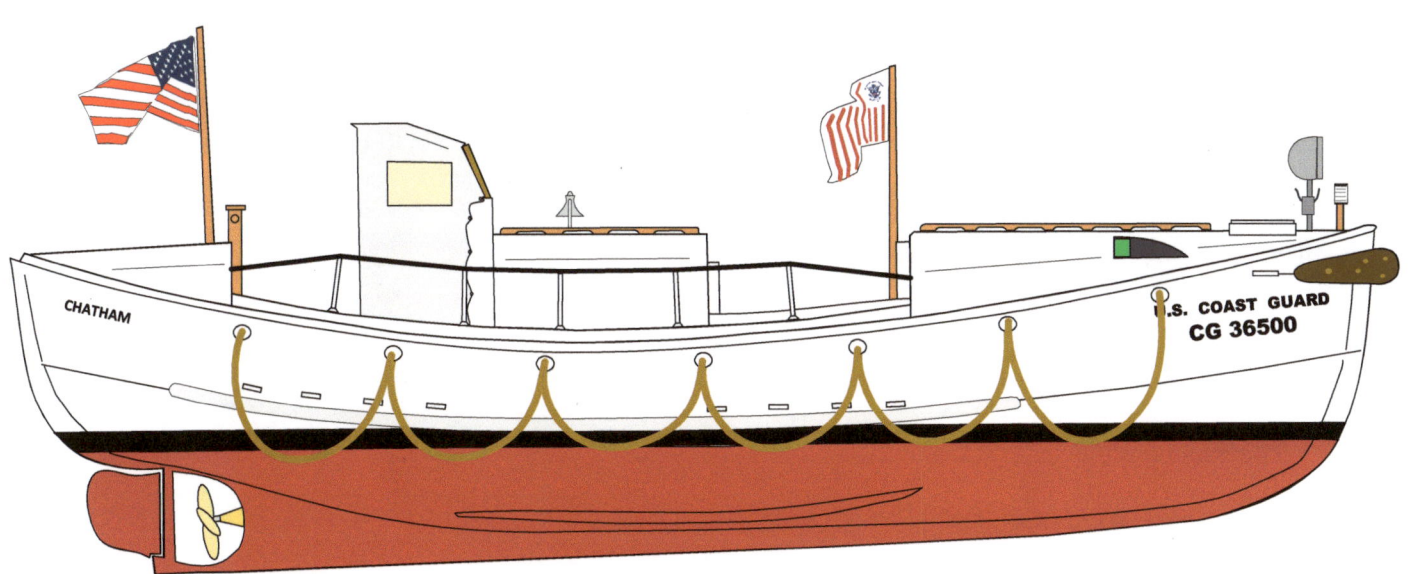

By Douglas R. Meier

Copyright © 2024
By Douglas R. Meier. This book or parts thereof may not be reproduced in any form, stored in any retrieval system, or transmitted in any form by any means—electronic, mechanical, photocopy, recording, or otherwise—without prior written permission of the publisher, except as provided by United States of America copyright law and fair use.

Although the author has made every effort to ensure that the information in this book was correct at press time, the author does not assume and hereby disclaims any liability to any party for any loss, damage, or disruption caused by errors or omissions, whether such errors or omissions result from negligence, accident, or any other cause.

A special thank you to the U.S. Coast Guard and CWO Roszkowski (Project officer) for the help with this book.

A special thank you to Jenna Loeser, Editor, Anisoara Hodoroaba, and Joe Robilio for their support.

All illustrations by Douglas R. Meier

U.S.C.G., U.S. Coast Guard, Coast Guard, the Coast Guard mark (racing stripe),
And the Coast Guard emblem are registered trademarks and are used with permission.

International Standard Book Number
ISBN: 979-8-218-40170-2

Semper Paratus (Always Ready)

We're always ready for the call,
We place our trust in Thee.
Through surf and storm and howling gale,
High shall our purpose be.
"Semper Paratus" is our guide,
Our fame, our glory too.
To fight to save or fight and die,
Aye! Coast Guard we are for you!

A verse from the song Semper Paratus
Words and Music by Captain Francis Saltus Van Boskerck, USCG

PREFACE

This started years ago while I was at sea. Drawing ships and boats, first on paper, then using a 2D program was a hobby of mine that filled the hours and days offshore.

The research for each drawing was fun and at the same time very frustrating. I was very surprised about the lack of information on some of our oldest and proudest boats or cutters. Most of the time it came down to a one-page mention on a Coast Guard web page or a fan page.

1970 to 2024 seemed to be the right era as it goes back about two generations. All the drawings are mine and I used any info that I could rustle up to complete them.

There are a few small craft that did not make it into the book simply because of lack of information available and space available. With a few exceptions, I tried to draw cutters and boats to show how they looked like after 1970.

I would like to think book is the most complete representation of the cutters and small boats from 1970 to 2024 available today.

A big thanks to the U.S. Coast Guard for its assistance in the completion of this book.

The flags cutters and small boats fly on a regular basis. History of the Coast Guard racing stripe

Coast Guard ensign. Flown at the mast 8 am to sunset while anchored or moored. Flown 24 hours a day underway.
This flag is a symbol of law enforcement authority.

The union jack. Flown at the bow staff from 8 am to sunset daily. Not flown while underway.

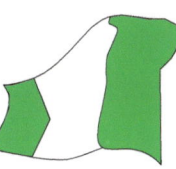

Senior command afloat. The highest-ranking officer in the harbor or on scene.

U.S. ensign. Flown from the stern staff while anchored or moored to a dock from 8 am to sunset daily. Flown from the masthead underway 24 hours a day while underway.

Commanding officer ashore. Not on cutter.

John F. Kennedy understood the importance of image-building and turned to French-born industrial designer Raymond Loewy to discuss improving the visual image of the federal government. Kennedy suggested the Coast Guard as an appropriate agency to start with. The overall design came to be known as the "Racing Stripe" or "Slash" emblem. On April 6, 1967, Commandant Edwin Roland ordered service-wide implementation of the Integrated Visual Identification System. The Racing Stripe received a public stamp of approval when CBS news anchor Walter Cronkite singled out the bark Eagle and its Racing Stripe logo with approving remarks.

TABLE OF CONTENTS

Ocean going cutters

		page
WMEC	125 ft. Active class	12
WMEC	143 ft. Sotoyono class	13
WMEC	180 ft. Cactus class	14
WMEC	180 ft. Cactus class	15
WMEC	205 ft. Cherokee class	16
WMEC	210 ft. Reliance class	17
WMEC	213 ft. Diver class	18
WMEC	230 ft. Storis	19
WHEC	255 ft. Owasco class	20
WMEC	270 ft. Famous class	21
WMEC	282 ft. Edenton class	22
WHEC	311 ft. Casco class	23
WHEC	327 ft. Treasury class	24
WHEC	387 ft. Hamilton class	25
WMSM	360 ft. Heritage class	26
WMSL	418 ft. Legend class	27

Icebreakers, polar, lake, harbor

		page
WYTL	65 ft. small harbor tug	28
WYT	85 ft Yard tug	29
WYTM	110 ft. tug	30
WTGB	140 ft. Bay class	31
WLBB	240 ft. Heavy icebreaker	32
WAGB	269 ft. Wind class	33
WAGB	290 ft Mackinaw	34
WAGB	309 ft. Glacier	35
WAGB	399 ft. Polar class	36
WAGB	418 ft. Healy	37

Patrol boats

WPBH	73 ft. Flagstaff	44
WPB	82 ft. Point class	45

Patrol boats

		page
WPB	82 ft. Point class squadron 1	46
WPB	87 ft. Protector class	47
WPB	95 ft. Cape class	48
WPB	110 ft. Island class	49
WSES	110 ft. Seabird class	50
WPB	123 ft. Island class	51
WPC	154 ft. Sentinel class	52
WPC	179 ft. Cyclone class	53

Training cutters

WIX	125 ft. Active class	54
WIX	180 ft. Gentian	55
WIX	295 ft. Eagle	56
WIX	338 ft. Courier	57

Motor Lifeboat, cutter boat, survey boat

MSB	25 ft. Motor surf boat SV	66
SRB	30 ft. Surf rescue craft	67
MLB	36 ft. Motor lifeboat	68
SPC-NLB	42 ft. Nearshore lifeboat	69
MLB	44 ft. Motor lifeboat	70
MLB	47 ft. Motor lifeboat	71
MLB	52 ft. Motor lifeboat	72
CB-ATON-M	18 ft. Aides to navigation boat	73
MCB	25 ft. Motor cargo boat	74
OTHB	26 ft. Over the horizon cutter boat	75
OTHB	26 ft. Over the horizon cutter boat	76
MSB	26 ft. Motor surf boat	77
LRI	35 ft. Long range interceptor	78
ASB	38 ft. arctic survey boat	79
ASB	39 ft. arctic survey boat	80

TABLE OF CONTENTS

Ports and waterways, utility, response, special purpose craft

		page
TPSB	25 ft. Security boat	84
RB-HS	25 ft. Homeland security boat	85
PSB	31 ft. Port security boat	86
TPSB	32 ft. Port security boat	87
PWB	32 ft. port & waterways boat	88
SPC-IRT	18ft. Ice rescue boat	89
SPC-IRT	21ft. Ice rescue boat	90
SPC-SW	24 ft. shallow water patrol craft	91
RB-HS	25 ft. Homeland security boat	92
PSD	27 ft. Presidential security	93
SPC-SW	27 ft. Shallow Water craft	94
RB-!!	29 ft. Response boat	95
UTB	30 ft. Utility boat medium M1	96
NSB	30 ft. Non standard boat	97
UTB	30 ft. Utility boat medium	98
SPCLE	33 ft. Law Enforcement boat	99
LARC	35 ft. Amphibious rescue craft	100
ACV	38 ft. air cushion vehicle	101
SPC-TB	38 ft. Training boat	102
UTB	40 ft. Utility boat medium	103
B	40 ft. Utility boat medium M IV	104
UTB	41 ft. Utility boat large	105
FCI	43 ft. Fast coastal interceptor	106
RB-M	45 ft. Response boat Medium	107
SPC-SV	64 ft. Special purpose craft	108

Aton boat, inland tender, coastal tender, seagoing tender, Construction tender

TANB	21 ft. Aton boat	112
TANB	26 ft. Aton boat	113
BU	45 ft. Buoy boat	114
BUSL	46 ft. Buoy boat	115

Aton boat, inland tender, coastal tender, seagoing tender, Construction tender

		page
BUSL	49 ft. Buoy utility boat	116
ANB	55 ft. Aton navigation boat	117
LCM	56 ft. cable laying landing craft	118
WLR	65 ft. construction tender	119
WLI	65 ft. inland buoy tender	120
WLV	128 ft. lightship	121
WLI	75 ft. inland construction tender	122
WLR	75 ft. river buoy tender	123
WLIC	100 ft. Cosmos class	124
WLI	100 ft. class C	125
WLIC	160 ft. Construction tender	126
WAGL	133 ft. White class	127
WLM	157 ft. Red class	128
WLM	175 ft. Hollyhock class	129
WLM	175 ft. Keeper class	130
WLB	180 ft. class A,B,C	131
WLB	225 ft. Juniper class	132

Helicopters

HH 52	Seaguard	138
H 3F	Pelican	140
H 60	Jayhawk	141
MH 65	Dolphin	143
MH 90	Enforcer	144
MH 68A	Stingray	146

Enlisted, Warrant, officer ranks

Insignias	148
Enlisted	149
Warrant officer	150
Commissioned officer	151

USCG classification symbols definitions

MLB	Motor Life Boat	WMSL	Maritime security cutter, large
SRB	Surf Rescue Boat	WMSM	Offshore Patrol Cutter
MSB	Motor Surfboat	WHEC	High endurance cutter
SPC-NLB	Near shore lifeboat	WMEC	Medium endurance cutter
UTB	Utility Boat	WPB	Patrol boat
UTL	Utility Boat, Light	WPC	Patrol cutter
RB-M	Response Boat-Medium	WSES	Surface effect ship
RB-S	Response Boat-Small	WPBH	Hydrofoil
DPB	Deployable Pursuit Boat		
SPC	Special Purpose Craft	WAGB	Polar icebreaker
SPC-LE	law enforcement craft	WLBB	Seagoing buoy tenders/ice breaker
SPC-TB	Training boat	WTGB	Icebreaking tugboat
SPC-IRT	Ice rescue boat	WYTL	Small ice breaking harbor tug
SPC-SV	Screening vessel	WYT	Yard tug
SPC-SW	Shallow water patrol craft		
RHIB	Rigid Hull Inflatable Boats	WIX	Training cutter
PSD	Presidential security boat		
FCI	Fast coastal interceptor	WLB	Seagoing buoy tender
NSB	Non standard boat	WLI	Inland buoy tenders
		WLIC	Inland construction tenders
ASB	Arctic Survey Boat	WLM	Coastal buoy tenders
BB-L	Cutter Boat Large	WLR	River buoy tenders
CB-M	Cutter Boat Medium		
CB-S	Cutter Boat Smal	ANB	Aids to Navigation Boats
CB-OTH	Over the Horizon boat	BU	Buoy Boat
TCB	Motor Cargo Boat	BUSL	Buoy Boat, Stern Loading
		ANB	Aids to Navigation Boat
PSB	Port security boat	ANLB	Aids to Navigation Logistics Boat
PWB	Ports and Waterways Boat	TANB	Trailered Aids to Navigation Boat
PWM	Ports and Waterways, Medium		
TPSB	Transportable Port Security Boat		

QUEEN OF THE FLEET

OLDEST COMMISSIONED CUTTER AWARD

This recognition was established to distinguish the Coast Guard Cutter as having served the fleet longest. The term Commissioned Cutter includes both commissioned and in-service cutters as defined by Coast Guard regulations. .

Eligibility Requirements. All "active, in commission" and "active, in service" Coast Guard cutters 65 feet and longer are eligible; this includes those cutters "in commission, special" and "in service, special." CGC EAGLE is specifically not eligible for recognition due to her special historical status.

The cutter with the earliest of active, in-commission or active, in-service date in the Coast Guard will be designated as the Oldest Commissioned Cutter and may be referred to colloquially as the "Queen of the Fleet."

The unit designated as the Oldest Commissioned Cutter will hold that distinction until it is placed in the status of "inactive, pending placement out of commission" or "inactive, pending placement out of service." Major shipyard renovation periods, during which a cutter is in a "Special" status, will not be subtracted from its accrued service time.

The queen of the fleet status started sometime in the 70's with the Campbell assuming the nick name "the queen of the fleet" or the "queen of the seas". The Coast guard made it official by authorizing the oldest cutter in commission to wear gold hull identification numbers and crew wearing gold numbers on their name tags.

Queen of the fleet past and current

Type	Number	Name	Years
WIX	157	Cuyahoga	Unofficial
WHEC	32	Campbell	1978 to 1982
WHEC	33	Duane	1982 to 1985
WHEC	35	Ingham	1985 to 1988
WLM	212	Fir	1988 to 1991
WMEC	38	Storis	1991 to 2007
WMEC	167	Acushnet	2007 to 2011
WLIC	315	Smilax	2011 to -

WMSL	maritime security cutter, large (national security cutters)
WMSM	Offshore Patrol Cutter
WHEC	high endurance cutter
WMEC	medium endurance cutter

A cutter is a Coast Guard vessel 65 feet or greater and designed for a crew to live aboard. Most cutters carry small boats including rigid hull inflatables, motor surf boats, survey boats and over the horizon boats that can operate independently from the cutter for extended periods. Major cutters have helicopter facilities including onboard hangers.

WAGB	Polar icebreaker
WLBB	Seagoing buoy tenders/ice breaker
WTGB	Icebreaking tugboat
WWYTL	Small ice breaking harbor tug
WYTM	Harbor tug
WYT	Harbor tug / yard tug

The Coast Guard has several types of icebreakers. The large seagoing class operate in the Arctic and Antarctic seas. The smaller icebreaking tugs and icebreaking harbor tugs operate in the Great lakes, large harbors and ports along the U.S. coastline. Some icebreakers are designed to do double duty and have provisions to service buoys. Some Buoy tenders are also built to operate as icebreakers.

125 FOOT ACTIVE CLASS PATROL BOAT (WMEC)

Builder	American Brown Boveri Electric Corporation, Camden, Nj
Cost	$63,173 (1927)
Built	1926–1927
Completed	35
Numbered	125 to 157

WIX-157 Cuyahoga
Queen of the fleet status

In service 1927 - 1978

Displacement	232 long tons
Length	125 ft Beam 23 ft 6 in Draft 7 ft 6 in
Propulsion	At launch: 2 × 6-cylinder, 300 hp Winton Model 114-6 diesel engines
	1938: 2 x Cooper-Bessemer EN-9 600 bhp diesel engines
Speed	Max 13 knots Cruise: 8 knots
Range	3,500 nm at max speed: 2,500 nmi
Complement	1938: 22 1944: 38 1960: 3 officers, 17 men
Armament	1927: 1 × 3"/27 caliber gun
	1941: 1 × 3"/23 caliber gun 2 × depth charge tracks, 10 depth charges
	1945: 1 × 40 mm/60 (single) 2 × 20 mm/70 (single) 2 × depth charge tracks
	2 × Mousetrap ASW
	1960: 1 × 40 mm/60

143 FOOT SOTOYOMO CLASS TUG (WMEC)

Builder Levingston Shipbuilding Co., Orange, TX
Commissioned in the U.S. Navy 14 February 1945
Transferred to the US Coast Guard 15 April 1959

In service 1959 - 1979

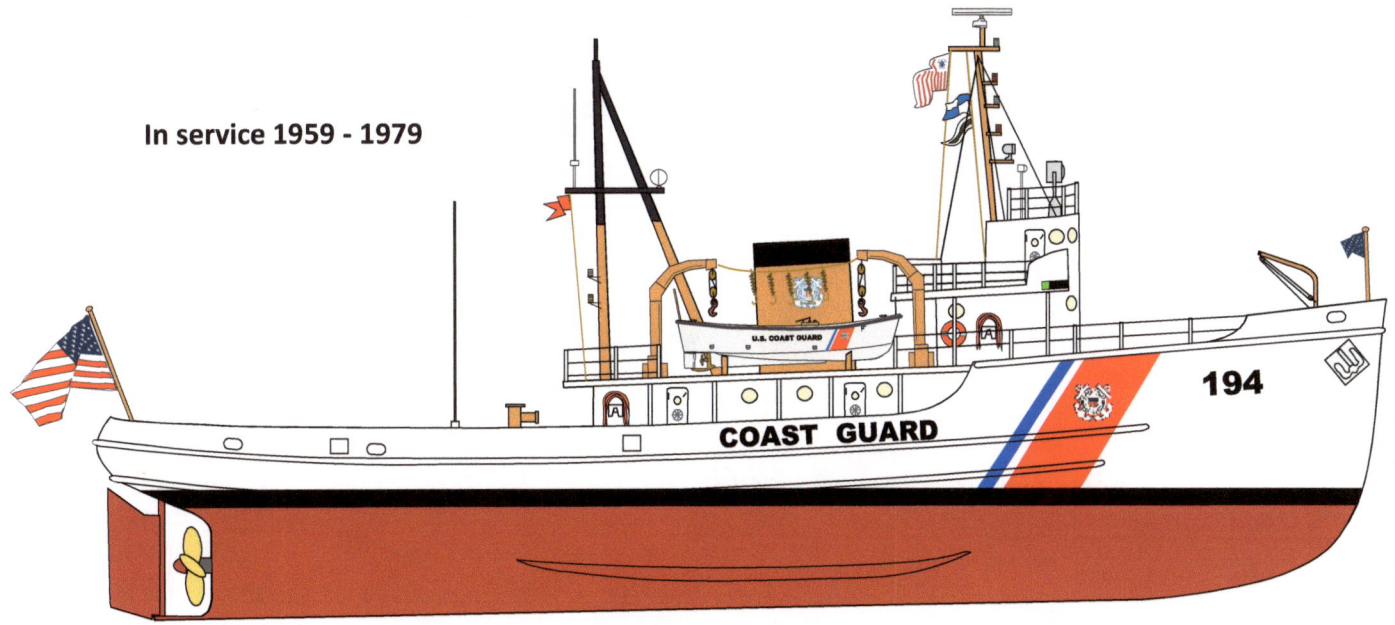

Displacement 534 t
Length 143 ft Beam 33 ft Draft 13 ft
Propulsion two GM 12-278A Diesel-electric engines
single Fairbanks Morse Main Reduction Gear
single propeller, 1,200shp
Fuel Capacity diesel 1,200
Speed 13 knots
Complement Officers 5 Enlisted 40
Armament one single 3 in (76 mm) dual purpose gun mount
two single 20 mm AA gun mounts

180 FOOT CACTUS-CLASS (WAGL-295/WLB-295/WAGO-295/WMEC-295)

Builder	Marine Ironworks & Shipbuilding Corporation, Duluth, Mn
Launched	3 July 1942
Cost	$871,946
WAGL	Light icebreaker (1942–1945)
WLB	Buoy tender (1945–1964)
WAGO	Oceanographic vessel (1964–1982)
WMEC	Medium endurance cutter (1982–1990)

Evergreen was the first dedicated oceanographic vessel in the Coast Guard's history. As an oceanographic vessel, she was also converted from a black-hull paint scheme to a white-hull paint scheme, which she wore until decommissioned.

In service 1943 - 1990

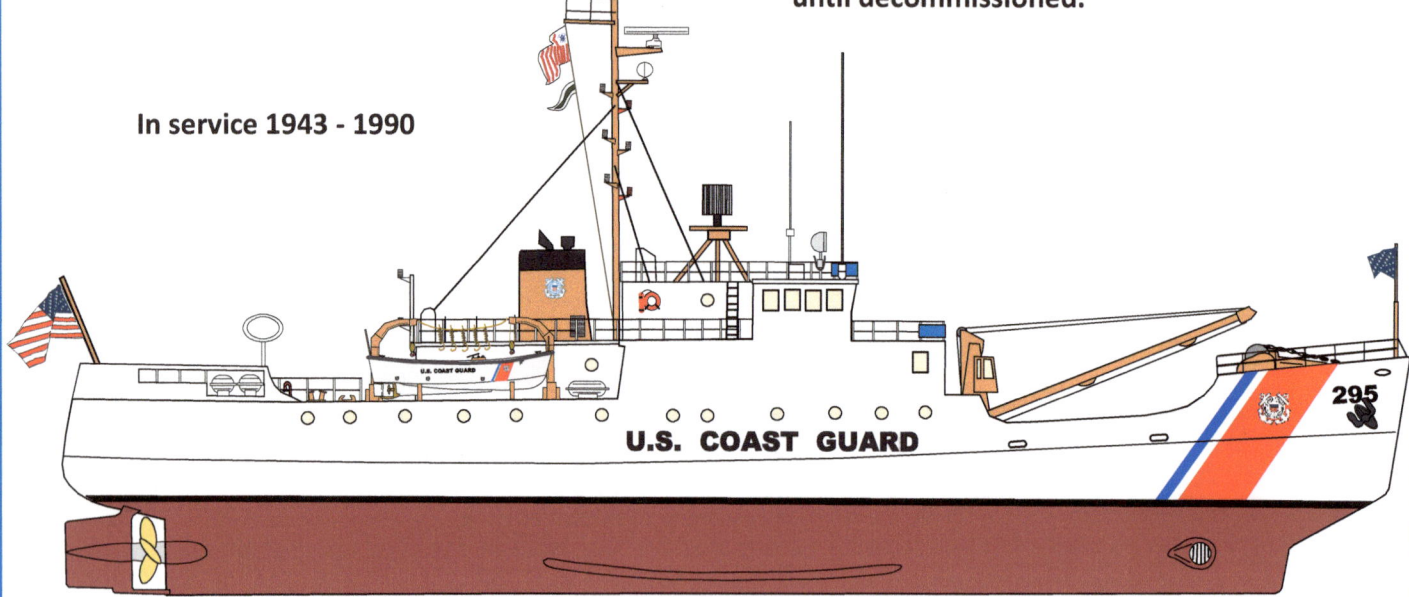

Displacement	935 long tons
Length	180 ft Beam 37 ft
Propulsion	2 × Westinghouse generators driven by 2 Cooper-Bessemer GND-8 8-cylinder 4-cycle 6352 cubic inch diesel engines
Speed	13 knots
Range	8,000 nmi at 13 knots
Complement	6 officers, 74 enlisted
Armament	20-mm guns, a 3-inch cannon, and depth charges

180 FOOT CACTUS CLASS (WMEC)

Builder	Marine Iron & Shipbuilding Corporation Duluth, MN
Commissioned	3 April 1943
Cost	$853,987

USCGC Citrus was a 180 ft WYB buoy tender converted to a WMEC in March 1979

In service 1943 - 1971

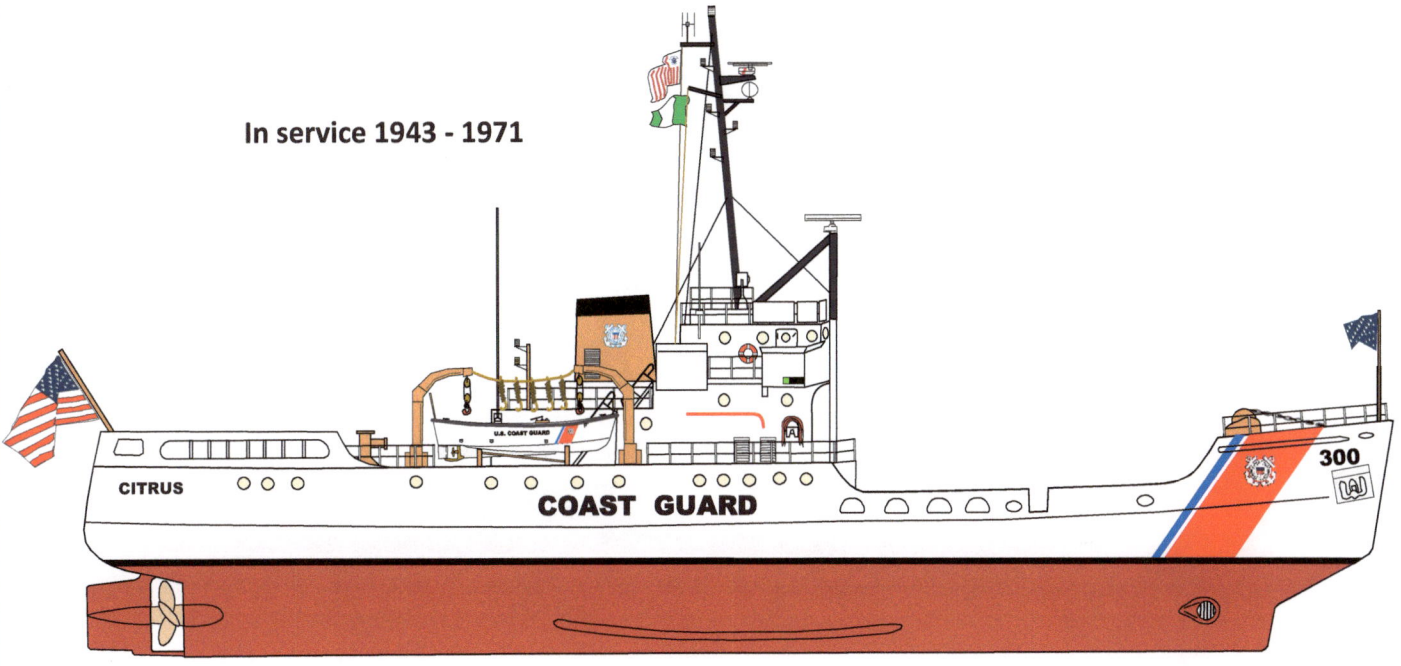

Displacement	1,026 long tons full load
Length	180 ft Beam 37 ft Draft 14.6 ft
Propulsion	1 electric motor connected to 2 Westinghouse generators driven by 2 Cooper-Bessemer-type GND-8, 4-cycle diesel engines; single screw
Speed	11.9 knots sustained 8.5 knots economic
Complement	4 officers, 2 warrants, 47 men

205 FOOT CHEROKEE-CLASS FLEET TUG (WMEC)

Builders For the Navy

Bethlehem Shipbuilding, Staten Island, NY
United Engineering Co, Alameda CA
Commercial Iron works, Portland OR
Charleston Shipbuilding, Charleston SC

Launched: 1929 – 1944

In service 1946 - 1994

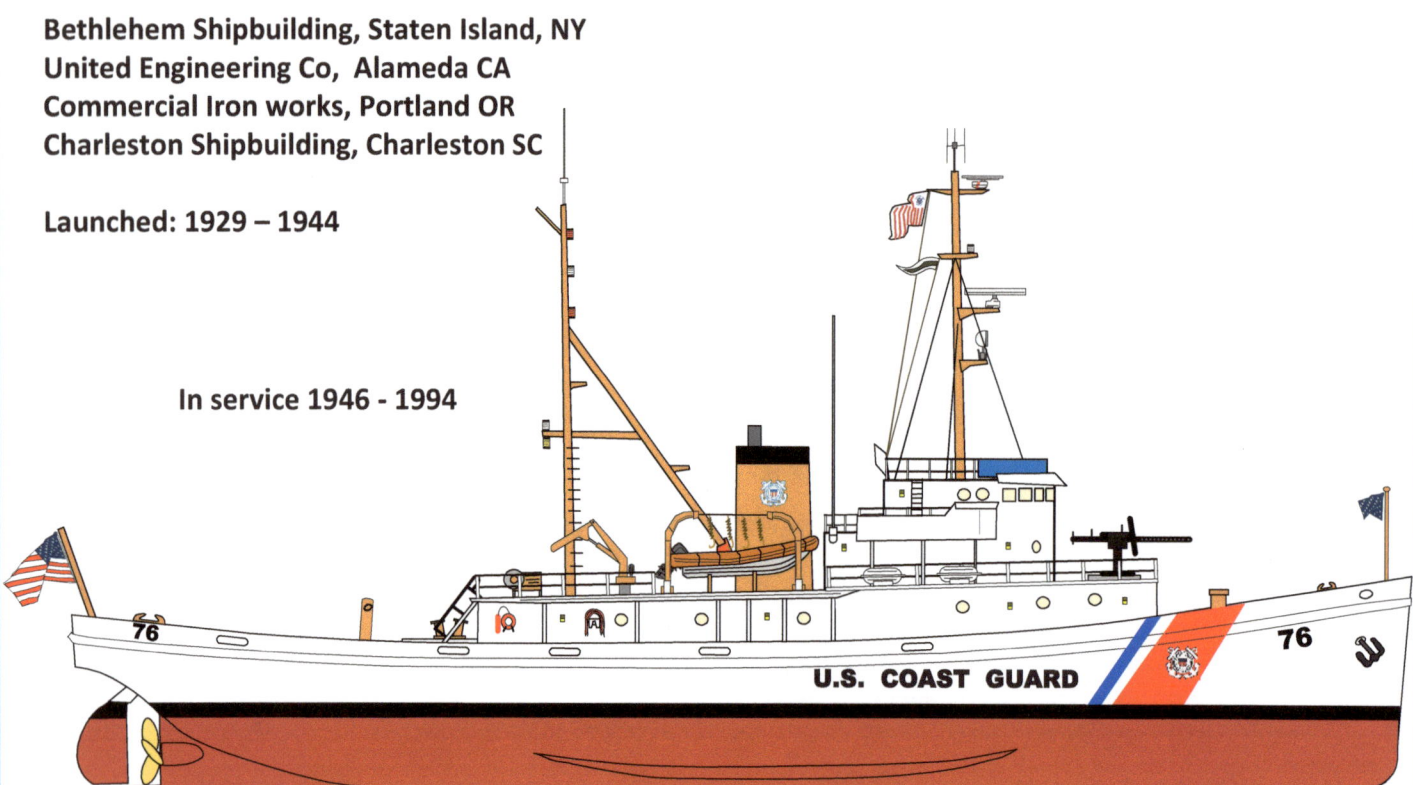

Displacement	1,641 tons
Length	205' 3" Beam: 38' 7" Draft: 16' 10"
Machinery	4 electric motors driven by 4 Allis Chalmers generators driven by 4 General Motors diesel engines; 3,000 BHP; single propeller
Fuel	97,581 gallons
Performance	Maximum Speed: 16.5 knots
	Economic/Cruising Speed: 10.1 knots
Range	13,097 mile range
Complement	7 officers, 1 warrant, 68 men
Armament	1 x 3"/50

210 FOOT RELIANCE CLASS (WMEC)

Builder	Todd Shipyards, Houston, Texas
	American Ship Building Company, Lorain, Ohio
	U.S. Coast Guard Yard, Curtis Bay, Maryland
	Christy Corporation, Sturgeon Bay, Wisconsin
original cost	$3.5 million
Built	1962–1968
Completed	16

In service 1964 - Current

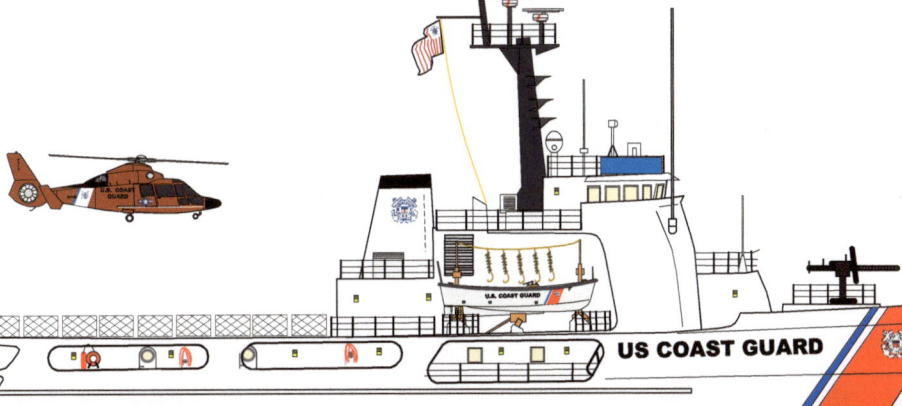

Displacement	1,127.2 long tons
Length	210 ft 6 in Beam 34 ft Draft 10 ft 9 in
Propulsion	2 × 2,500 hp ALCO 251B diesel
Speed	18 knots
Range	8,000 nm at 12 knots
Complement	75
Armament	1 × 25mm Mk 38 autocannon
	2 × M2HB .50 caliber machine guns
Aviation facilities	Helipad

213 FOOT DIVER-CLASS (WMEC)

Built as USS Shackle US Navy
Builder Basalt Rock Company, Napa, Ca
Launched 1 April 1943

WMEC-167 Acushnet
Queen of the fleet status 2007

Transferred to the Coast Guard 1946
WMEC 167
WMEC 168
WMEC 6

In service 1946 - 2011

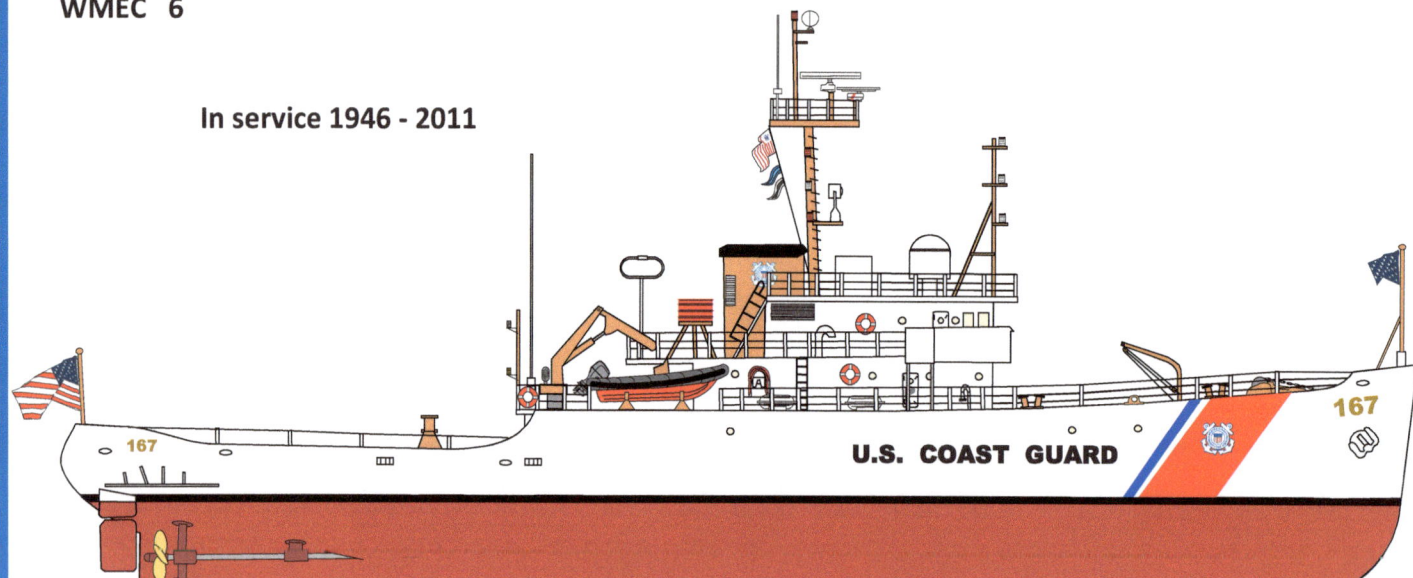

Displacement 1,720 long tons
Length 213 ft 6 in Beam 39 ft Draught 14 ft 4 in
Propulsion Diesel-electric, four Fairbanks-Morse 6-cylinder opposed piston engines driving four generators and motors, driving two shafts with 3,460 shp
Speed 15 knots
Boats carried 2
Crew 75
Armament two 40 mm AA gun mounts; four .50 cal. machine guns

230 FOOT STORIS CLASS (WAGL-38/WAG-38/WAGB-38/WMEC-38)

Builder   Toledo Shipbuilding Company, Toledo, Ohio
Launched   4 April 1942
Cost $2,072,889 USD

WMEC-38 Storis
Queen of the fleet status 1991

In service 1942 - 2007

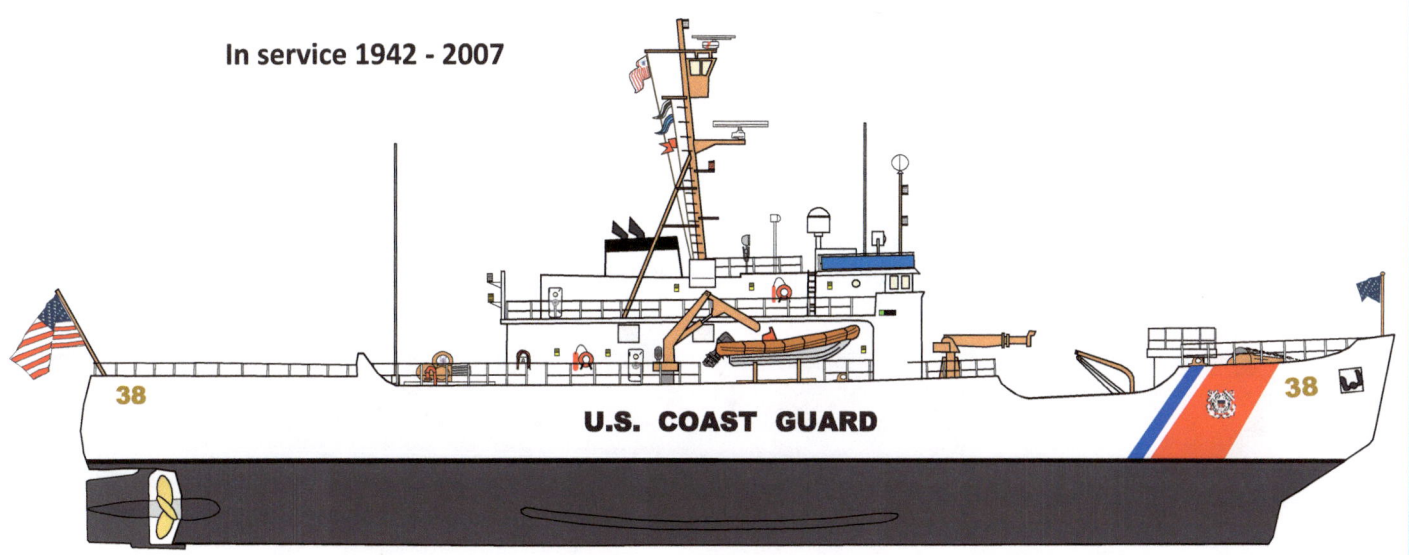

Displacement   2,030 long tons
Length   230 ft Beam 43 ft 2 in Draft 15 ft
Propulsion   Diesel-electric
Speed   14 knots
Range   22,000 mi
Complement   12 officers; 72 enlisted
Armament   1 × 25mm Mk 38 MOD 0 gun
                      2 × .50 cal M2 Browning machine guns

255 FOOT OWASCO-CLASS (WHEC)

Builders Western Pipe & Steel San Francisco, CA
US Coast Guard Yard
Built 1944–1946
Completed 13

In service 1945 - 1974

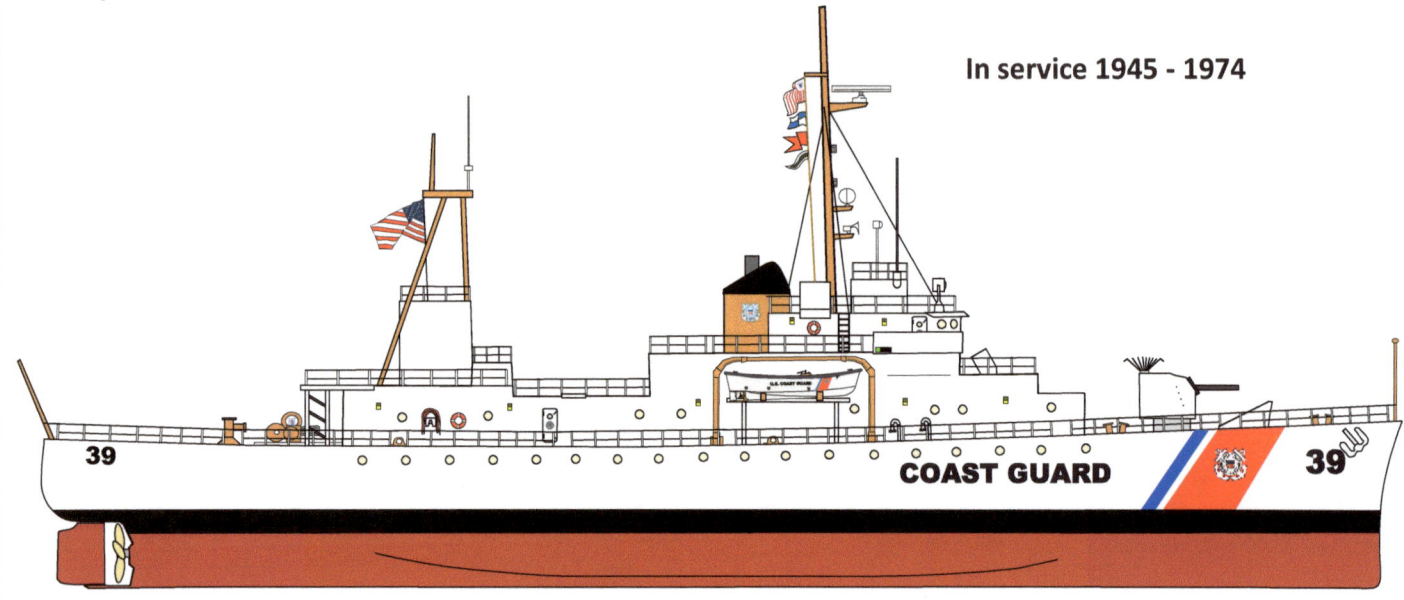

Displacement	1,978 full
Length	254 ft Beam 43 ft 1 in Draft 17 ft 3 in
Installed power	4,000 shp
Propulsion	1 x Westinghouse electric motor driven by a turbine
Fuel capacity	141,755 gal (95%)
Speed	17 knots
Range	6,157 mi at 17 knots 10,376 mi at 10 knots
Complement	10 officers, 3 warrants, 130 enlisted
Armament	1945, 2 x twin 5 in/38 cal. dual purpose gun mounts
	2 x quad 40 mm AA gun mounts
	2 x depth charge tracks
	6 x "K" gun depth charge projectors
	1 x Hedgehog projector

270 FOOT FAMOUS CLASS (WMEC)

Builders Robert Derecktor Shipyard Middletown, RI
Tacoma Boatbuilding Company, Tacoma, WA

Cost 37.1 million to 42 million

Built 1979–1989

Completed 13

In service 1983 - Current

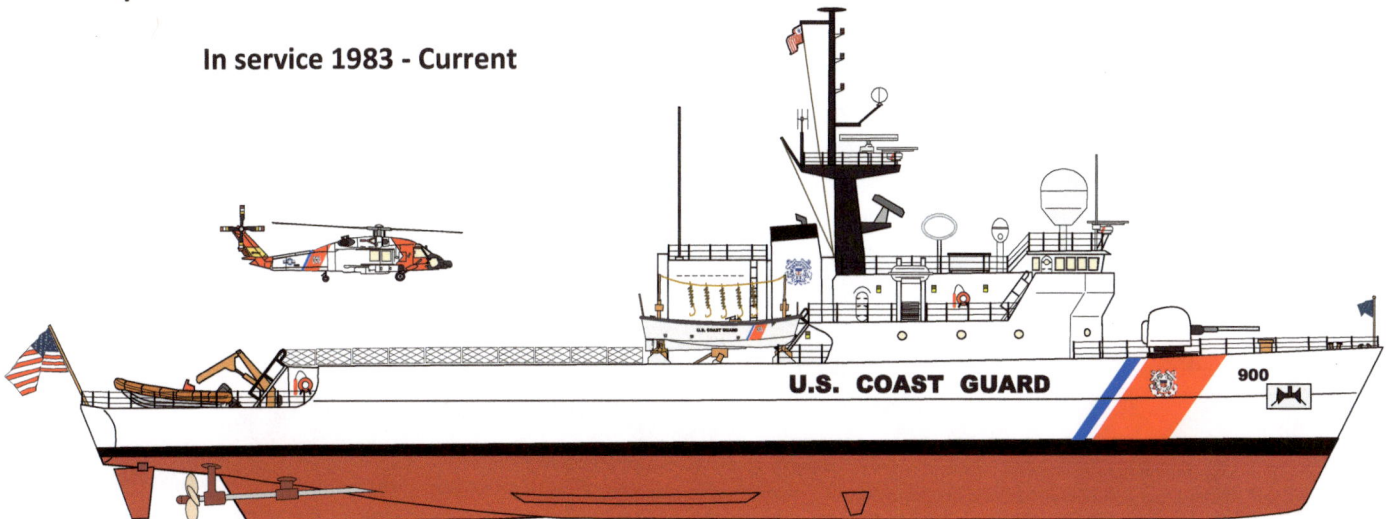

Displacement	1,800 long tons
Length	270 ft Beam 38 ft Draft 14 ft 5 in
Propulsion	2 × turbo-charged ALCO V-18 diesel engines
	2 × 9-foot-diameter controllable pitch propellers
	2 × Caterpillar V12 diesel generators
Speed	19.5 knots
Range	9,900 nm
Complement	100 (14 officers, 86 enlisted)
Armament	1 × OTO Melara Mark 75 76 mm/62 caliber naval gun
	2 × .50 caliber (12.7 mm) machine guns
Aviation facilities	Helipad and hangar for HH-65 Dolphin or HH-60J Jayhawk

282 FOOT EDENTON-CLASS SALVAGE AND RESCUE SHIP (WMEC)

Builders   Brooke Marine lake lothing, UK
Launched as   USN Edenton 15 May 1968

Transferred to the Coast Guard as
USCGC Alex Haley (WMEC-39), 1999

In service 1999 - Current

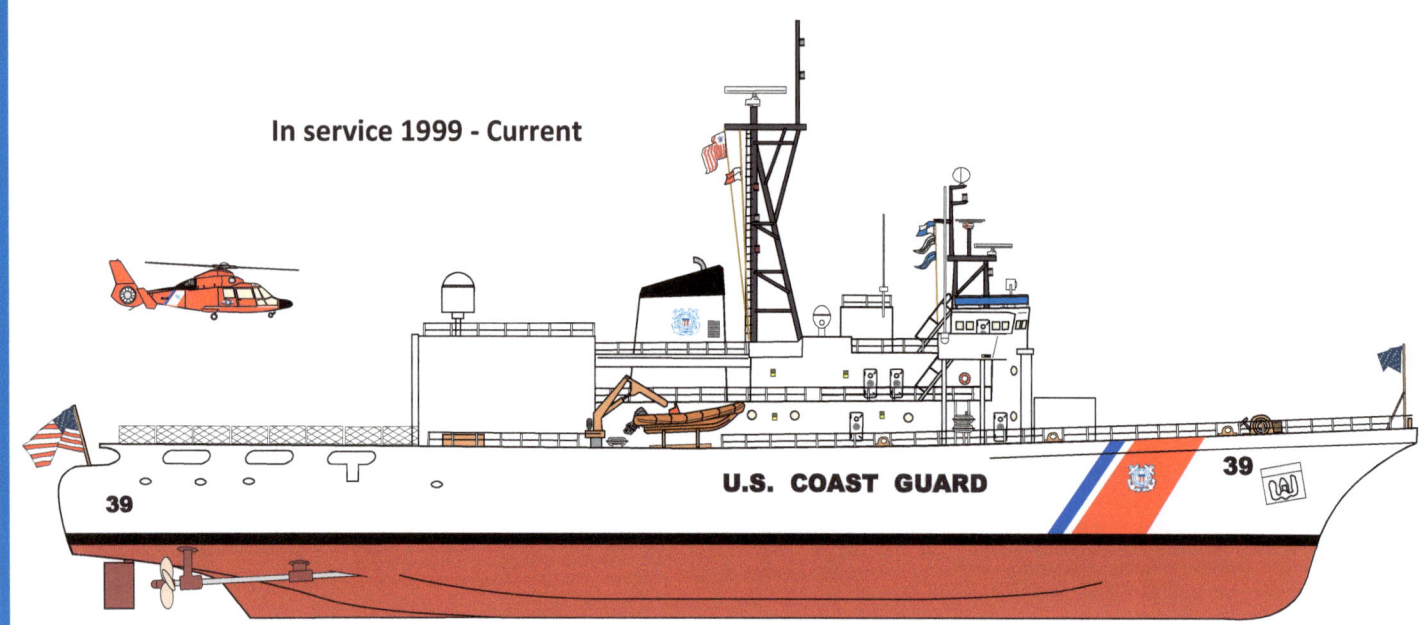

Displacement 2,592 tons
Length   282.67 ft Beam 59 ft Draft 17 ft, 18 ft max
Propulsion   4 Caterpillar diesel engines, 6,800 shp. twin screws
Speed   18 knots
Range   10,000 miles
Complement   10 officers 90 enlisted 4 aircrew
Armament   2 × Mk 38 Mod 2 25 mm Machine Gun Systems
              2 × 0.5 in guns

311 FOOT CASCO CLASS (WHEC)

Builders	Puget Sound Navy Yard, Bremerton, Wa (3 ships)
	Boston Navy Yard, Boston, Ma (2 ships)
	Lake Washington Shipyard, Houghton, Wa (10 ships)
	Associated Shipbuilders, Inc., Seattle, Wa (3 ships)
Built	October 1939-November 1944
Completed	18

Transferred from the Navy to the Coast Guard In service 1946 - 1988
Numbered 370 to 387

Displacement	2,040 tons standard 2,551 tons full load
Length	310 ft 9 in Beam 41 ft 1 in Draft 12 ft 5 in
Installed power	6,000 to 6,080 horsepower
Propulsion	Diesel engine, two shafts
Speed	18 knots
Range	20,000 nm at 12 knots
Complement	151
Armament	1 × 5-inch gun
	2 × twin 40--millimeter gun mounts 2 twin 40--millimeter gun mounts
	2 twin 20-mm antiaircraft gun mounts (removed 1957)
	1 Hedgehog Mark 10
	4 depth charge projectors
	Triple 12.75-inch antisubmarine warfare torpedo tubes fitted mid-1960s

327 FOOT TREASURY CLASS (WHEC)

Shipbuilder   Philadelphia Navy Yard
              Charleston Naval Yard
              Brooklyn Navy Yard
Built   7   1936 – 1937
Cost $2.5 million each

WHEC-32 Campbell
Queen of the fleet status 1978

WHEC-33 Duane
Queen of the fleet status 1982

WHEC-35 Ingham
Queen of the fleet status 1985

In service 1936 - 1988

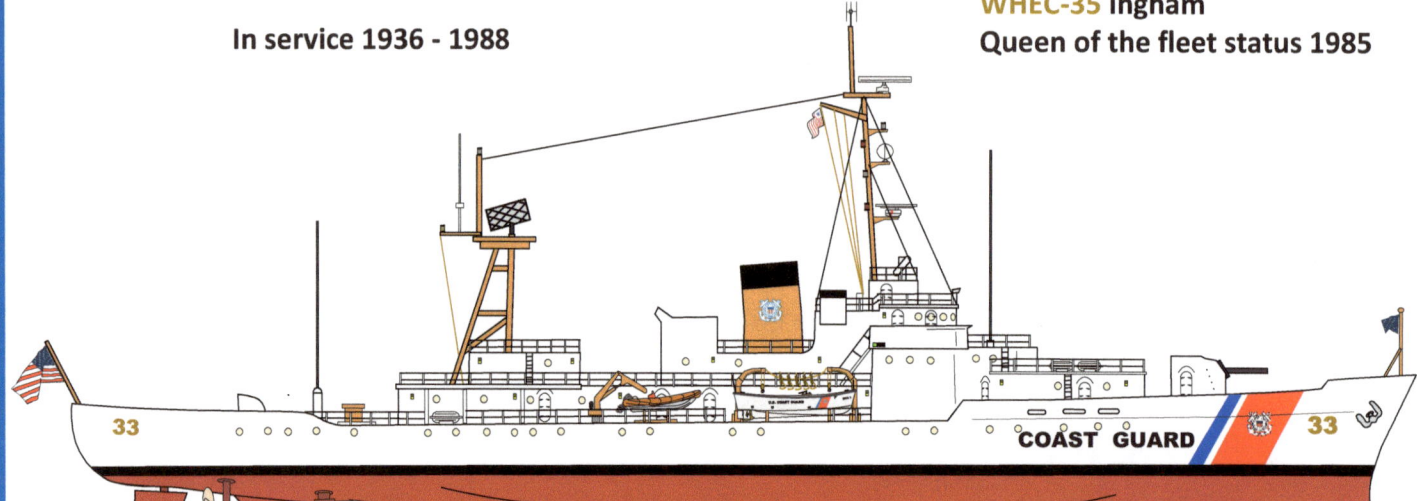

Displacement	2,216 long tons
Length	327 ft Beam 41 ft Draught 12.5 ft
Propulsion	2 × oil-fueled Babcock & Wilcox boilers
	Westinghouse geared turbines 2 shafts 6,200 hp
Speed	20 knots
Range	12,300 nautical miles at 11 knots
Complement	125
Armament	2 × 5 in / 51 cal. guns
	2 × 6-pounder guns 8 × .5-inch machine guns
	Aircraft carried 1 x Grumman JF-2 Duck or Curtiss SOC-4

360 FOOT HERITAGE-CLASS (WMSM)

Builder　　　　　Eastern Shipbuilding, Austal USA
Planned　　　　 11 (possibly up to 25)
First ship to be delivered late 2024

Displacement	3,700 long tons
Length	360 ft Beam 54 ft Draft 17 ft
Installed power	4 x 940 eKW diesel generators
Propulsion	2 × 9,760 hp Fairbanks Morse 16V28/33D STC diesel engines at 1,000 rpm
Speed	24.5 knots
Range	10,200 nm at 14 knots
Endurance	60 days
Boats carried	3 x Over-the-horizon boats
Complement	126
Armament	1 x MK 110 57 mm gun a variant of the Bofors 57 mm gun and Gunfire Control System
	1 x BAE Systems Mk 38 Mod 3 25 mm gun with 7.62 mm co-axial gun[3]
	2 x M2 Browning .50 caliber (12.7 mm) machine guns mounted on a MK 50 Stabilized Small Arms Mount (SSAM)
	4 x crew-served M2 Browning .50 caliber (12.7 mm) machine guns
	Armor Ballistic protection over critical areas and main gun
Aircraft carried	One MH-60 or MH-65, plus sUAS
Aviation facilities	Flight deck, hangar for all aircraft

378 FOOT HAMILTON CLASS (WHEC)

Builders	Avondale Shipyards
Built	1965–1972
Completed	12
Aircraft carried	1 × MH-65 Helicopter
Aviation facilities	Flight deck and Hangar

In service 1967 - 2021

Displacement	3,250 metric tons
Length	378 ft Beam 43 ft Draft 15 ft
Installed power	2 × 550KW GM 8-645 diesel generators
	1 × 500KW Solar Model 101506-2001 gas generator
Propulsion	CODOG system 2 × Fairbanks-Morse 38TD8-1/8-12 12-cylinder diesel engines generating 7,000 hp and 2 × Pratt & Whittney FT4A-6 gas turbines producing 36,000 hp
Speed	29 knots
Range	14,000 nm
Endurance	45 days
Complement	167 and can carry up to 186
Armament	1 × OTO Melara Mark 75 76 mm/62 caliber naval gun 2 × 25 mm Mk38
	1 × MK 15 Block 1 20 mm Phalanx CIWS 6 × .50 caliber machine guns

418 FOOT LEGEND CLASS (WMSL)

Builders	Ingalls Shipbuilding	Aircraft carried	1 × MH-65C Dolphin MCH and 2 × sUAS
		Aviation facilities	50-by-80-foot flight deck, hangar for all aircraft
Cost	$670m to $735m		
Completed	10		
Planned	11 (Option for 12th)		

In service 2008 - Current

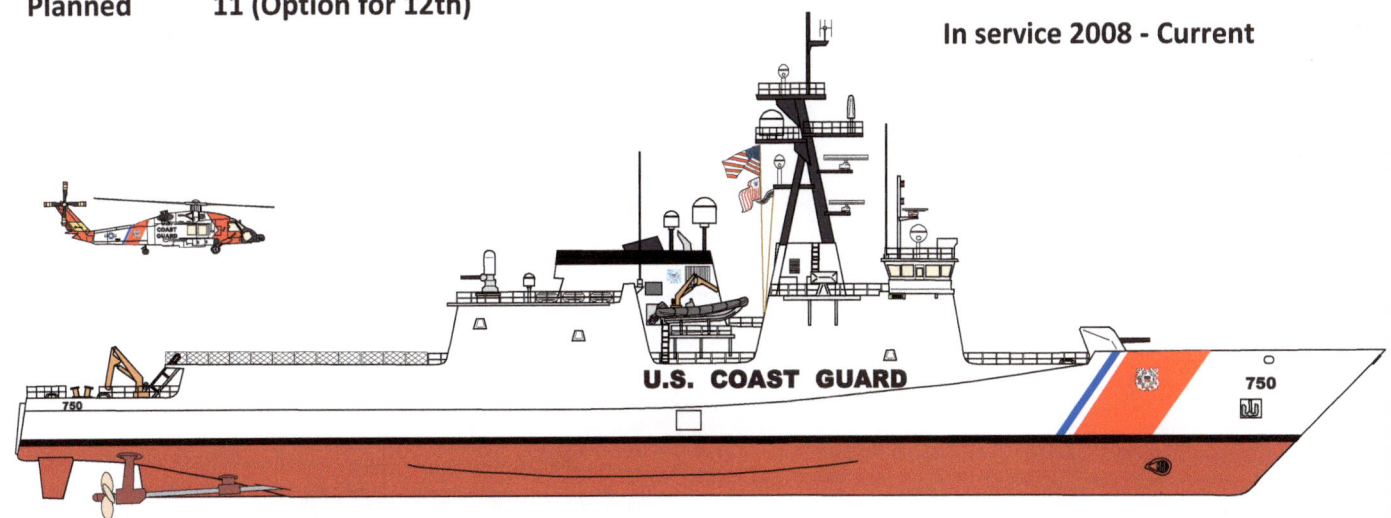

Displacement	4,500 long tons
Length	418 feet Beam 54 feet Draft 22.5 feet
Installed power	3 × Caterpillar 3512B diesel generators
Propulsion	combined diesel and gas
	2 × 9,900 hp MTU 20V 1163 diesels
	1 × 30,000 hp GE LM2500 gas turbine engine
Speed	Over 28 knots
Range	12,000 nautical miles
Complement	113 (14 officers + 99 enlisted) and can carry up to 148 depending on mission
Armament	1 × Mk 110 57mm gun a variant of the Bofors 57 mm gun and Gunfire Control System
	1 × 20 mm Block 1B Baseline 2 Phalanx Close-In Weapons System
	4 × crew-served .50 caliber (12.7 mm) Browning M2 machine guns
	2 × crew-served M240B 7.62 mm machine guns
	Designed for but not with additional weapons and sensors
	Armor Ballistic protection for main gun

65 FOOT SMALL HARBOR TUG (WYTL)

Builders	Gibbs Gas Engine, 1961–62
	Barbour Boat Works, 1962–1963
	Western Boat Builders, 1966–1967
Built	1961–1967
Cost	158,336.00 1961
Completed	15

Icebreaking capabilities

18 in of ice with propulsion ahead
21 in of ice backing and ramming

Operating only from Maine to Virginia.

In service 1961 - Current

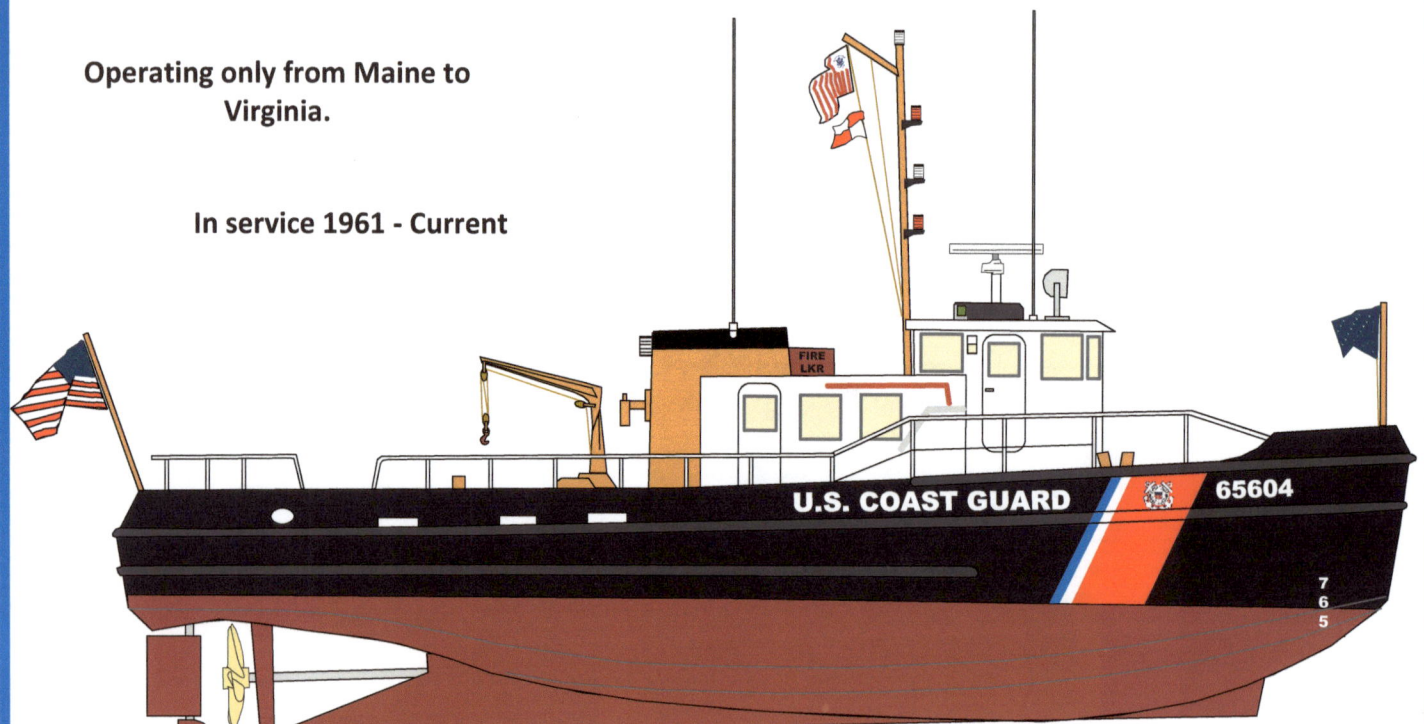

Displacement	74 tons
Length	64 ft 11 in Beam 19 ft 1 in Draft 9 ft max
Propulsion	400 hp diesel, single screw
Speed	10.6 knots max (1964)
Range	1,130 miles at 10.6 kts
	3,690 miles at 7.0 kts (1964)
Complement	5 men

85 FOOT ST CLASS HARBOR TUG (WYT)

Delivered to the US Army Quartermasters Corps in Sept 1945

Commissioned by Coast Guard mid 1950's

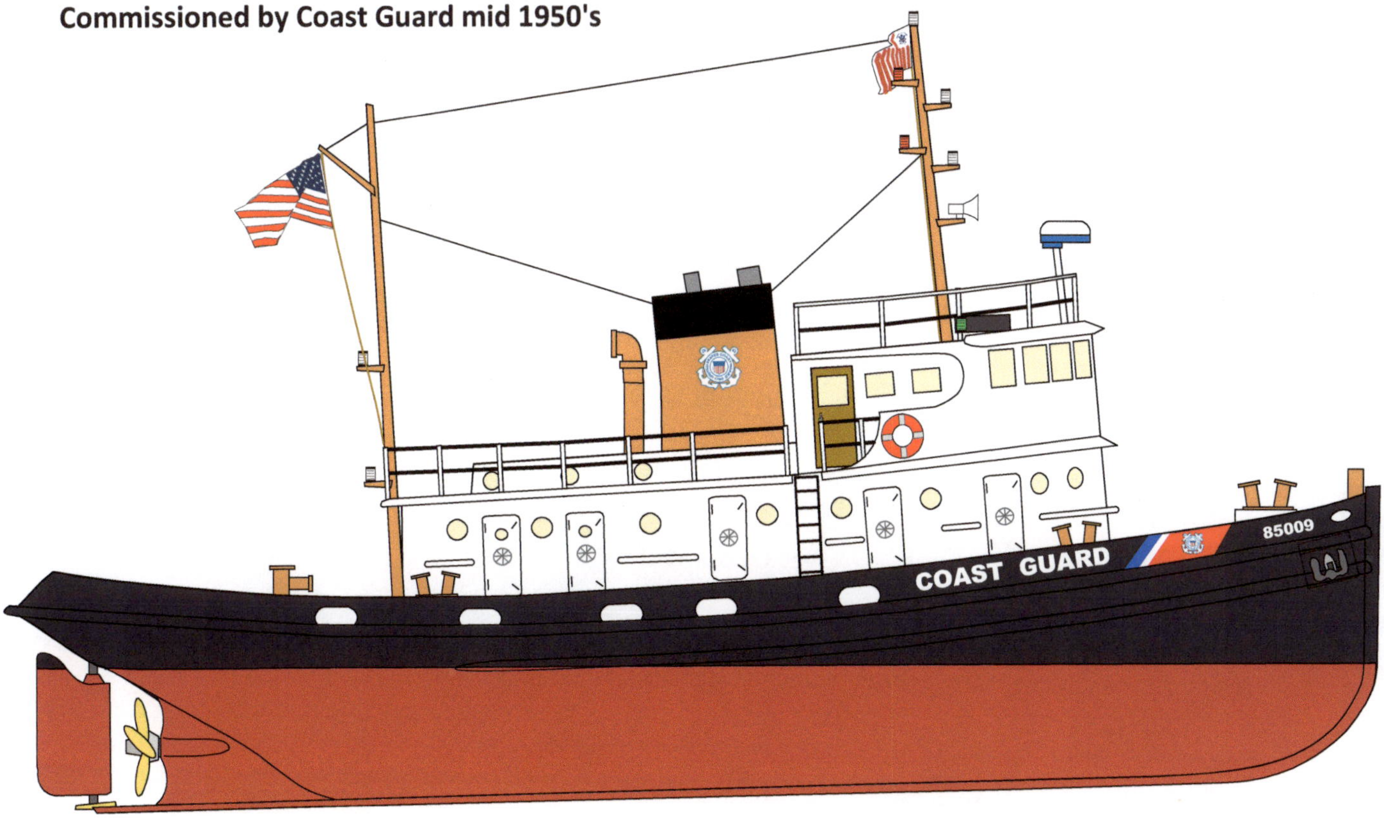

Builder Equitable Equipment, Madisonville, LA.
Cost 300,000.00

Stationed at the Coast Guard Curtis Bay yard her entire career, CGC Messenger (85009) performed harbor duties, ship assist, and ship docking duties.

Displacement	140 gross tons
Length	86'
Beam	23'
Draft	10'
Speed	9.5 kts
Propulsion	1 8cyl Enterprise diesel type DMG-38, diesel engine, 650bhp.

110 FOOT ARUNDEL / MANITOU / APALACHEE CLASS TUG (WYTM)

Builders	Gulfport Works, Port Arthur, Tx
	Defoe Boat Works, Bay City, Mi
	Coast Guard Yard Curtis Bay MD
Cost	$309,000
Built	Arundel class 4
	Manitou class 2
	Apalachee class 7

Ice breaking capacity

capable of breaking ice up to 3 ft thick

In service 1939 - 1988

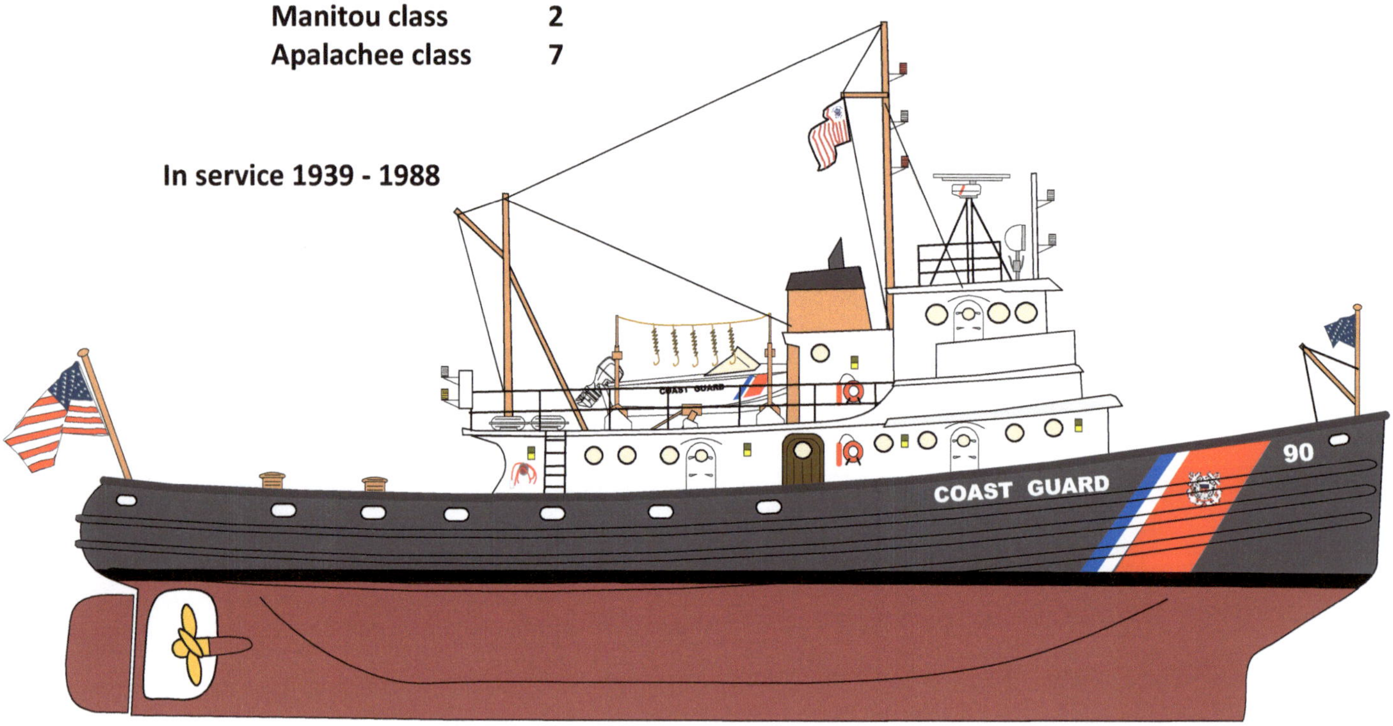

Displacement 328 tons
Length   110 ft Beam 26 ft 5 in Draft 12 ft
Power   1 × Westinghouse electric motor with 2 x Westinghouse generators
          2 x 8-567A GM diesels, 1,000 SHP
Speed   11.2 knots max 8.0 knots cruise
Range   2,000 nm at cruise
Complement 1 warrant, 19 enlisted

140 FOOT BAY-CLASS TUGBOAT (WTGB)

Builders Tacoma Boatbuilding Company, Tacoma, Wa
Bay City Marine Incorporated, National City, Ca

Built 1977-1987 Completed 9

In service 1979 - Current

Ice breaking capacity

fresh water ice up to 20 inches thick, and break ice up to 3 feet thick, through ramming. Ram pressure ridges of up to eight feet in thickness

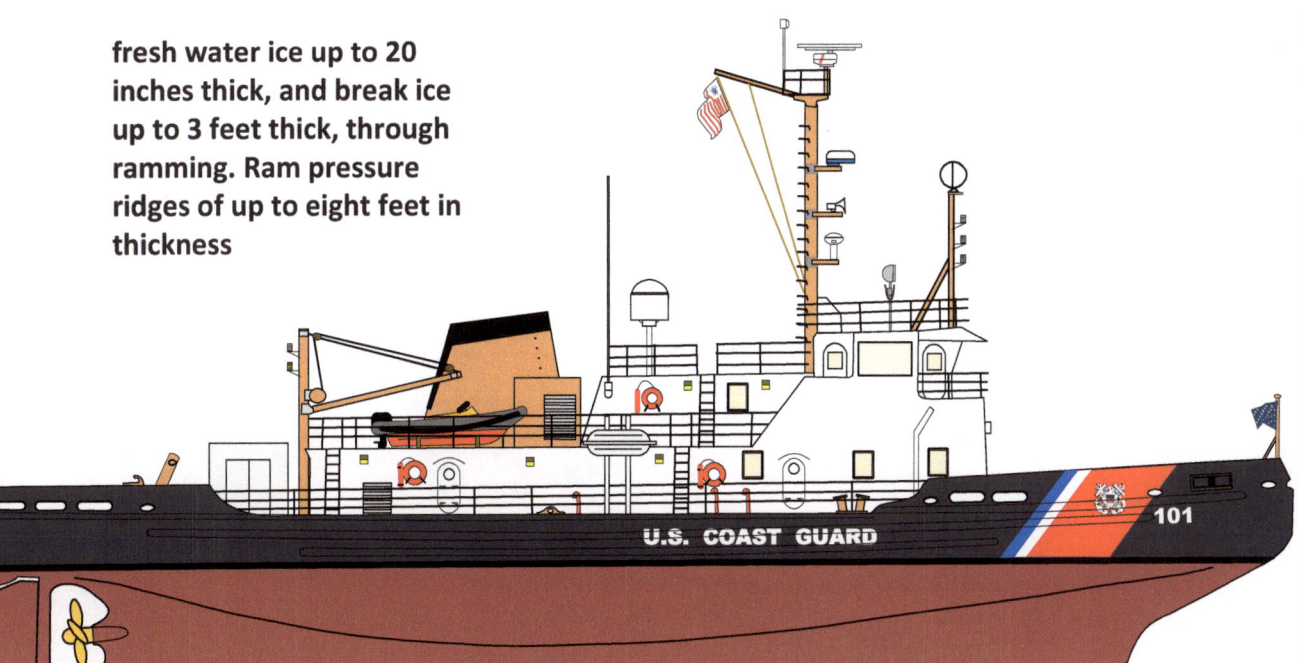

Displacement 662 tons
Length 140 ft Beam 37 ft 5 in Draught 12 ft 6 in
Propulsion diesel electric: 2 Fairbanks Morse diesel engines with Westinghouse DC generators, 1 Westinghouse DC motor
Speed 14.7 knots
Range 1,500 nautical miles at 14.7 knots 3,500 nautical miles at 12 knots 6,000 nautical miles at 10 knots
Complement 17 (3 officers)
Armament 2 × M240 machine guns

240 FOOT HEAVY ICEBREAKER MACKINAW (WLBB-30)

Builder Marinette Marine Corporation Marinette, Wi
Commissioned June 10, 2006

Homeport Cheboygan, Michigan

Ice breaking capacity

Freshwater ice up to 32 inches thick at 3 knots 14 inches at 10 knots.
Smooth, continuous ice up to 42 inches thick by rising on top of it and crushing it with the weight of her bow.

In service 2006 - Current

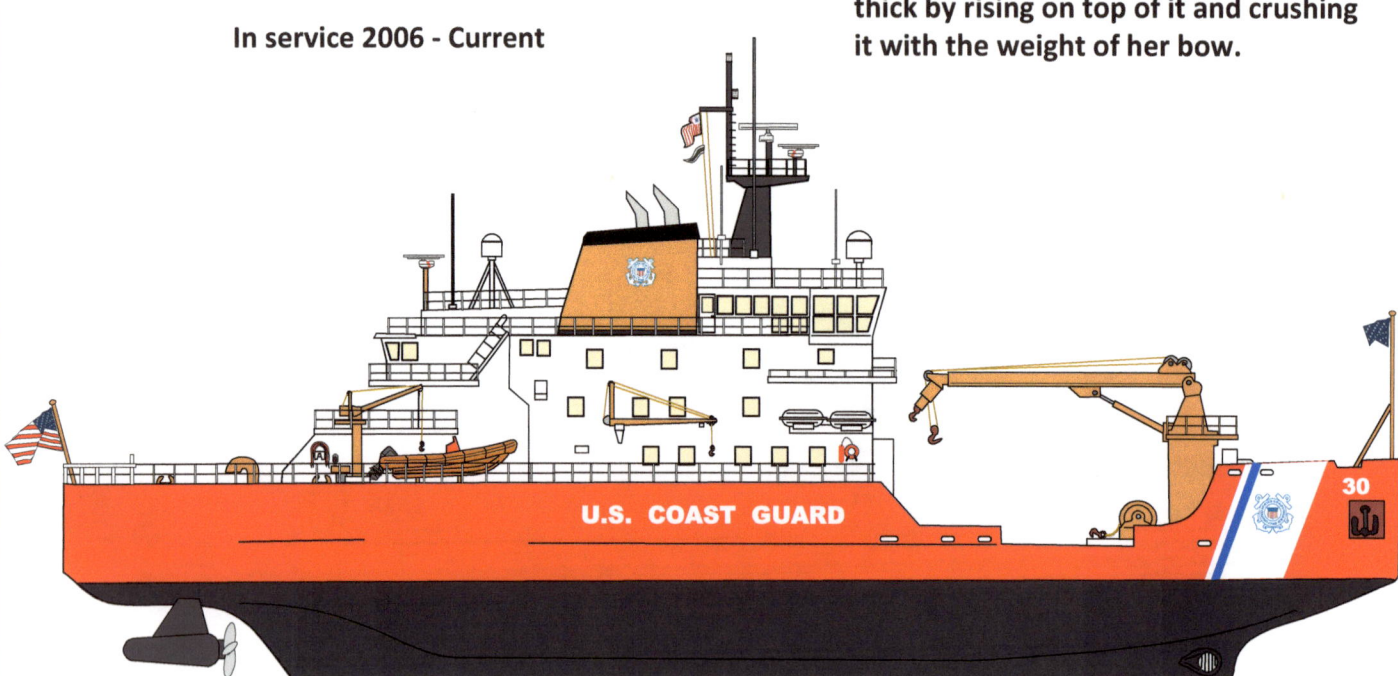

Displacement	3,500 tons
Length	240 ft Beam 58.5 ft Draft 16 ft
Propulsion	Integrated Main Propulsion & Electrical Plant 9,119 shp
	ABB Azipod - Fixed Pitch, 10' diameter
	550 hp bow thruster
Fuel	130,896 US gal
Speed	16 knots
Range	at 12 knots, 4,000 nm
Complement	9 Officers, 46 Enlisted
Armament	2 x machine guns Various small arms

269 FOOT WIND CLASS ICEBREAKER (WAGB)

Builders	Western Pipe and Steel Company, San Pedro, CA
Built	1942–1946
Cost	10 million each
Built	7

Ice breaking capacity

Ramming ice up to 6 ft. thick at a rate of 75 ft. per ram

In service 1944 - 1989

1975, the remaining white Wind class cutters were painted red for improved Arctic visibility

Displacement	6,515 tons
Length:	269 ft Beam: 63 ft 6 in Draft: 25 ft 9 in max
Installed power	Four 3,000 horsepower DeLaval diesel engines, two GE electric motors Westinghouse DC electric motor driving bow propeller.
Speed:	Top speed: 13.4 knots Economic speed: 11.6 knots
Range:	32,485 nautical miles
Complement:	14 officers, 137 crew + room for 12 scientists and 14 AvDet personnel
Aircraft carried:	two helicopters in telescoping hangar

309 FOOT ICEBREAKER GLACIER (WAGB)

Builder	Ingalls Shipbuilding, Pascagoula, MS for the U.S. Navy
Commissioned	27 May 1955
Transferred to the United States Coast Guard, 30 June 1966	

In service 1966 - 1987

1973, painted red for improved Arctic visibility

Aircraft carried	2 helicopters.
Air detachment	4 officers/pilots and 10 enlisted
Aviation facilities	Flight deck with retractable hangar, and overhead crane for aircraft engine service

Ice breaking capacity

Ramming ice up to 20 ft. thick
4 ft. at 3 knots continuous

Displacement	8,449 long tons full load
Length	309 ft 6 in Beam 74 ft Draft 29 ft
Propulsion	Diesel-electric 10 × Fairbanks-Morse diesels
	2 × Westinghouse electric motors 21,000 shp 2 shafts
Speed	17.6 knots
Range	29,200 nautical miles at 12 knots
Boats & landing craft	4 lifeboats, 1 LCVP, and 1 Arctic Survey Boat
Complement	14 officers, 2 warrant officers, 225 enlisted
Armament	1 × twin 5 in (130 mm) guns 3 × twin 3 in guns 4 × 20 mm guns

290 FOOT ICEBREAKER MACKINAW (WAGB)

Builder	Toledo Shipbuilding Company, American Ship Building Company
Commissioned	December 20, 1944
Cost	10 million

1998, Mackinaw was painted red for improved visibility

Icebreaking capacity

up to 42 inches of solid "blue" ice
up to 38 to 40 feet of shattered, heaped-up "windrow" ice

In service 1944 - 2006

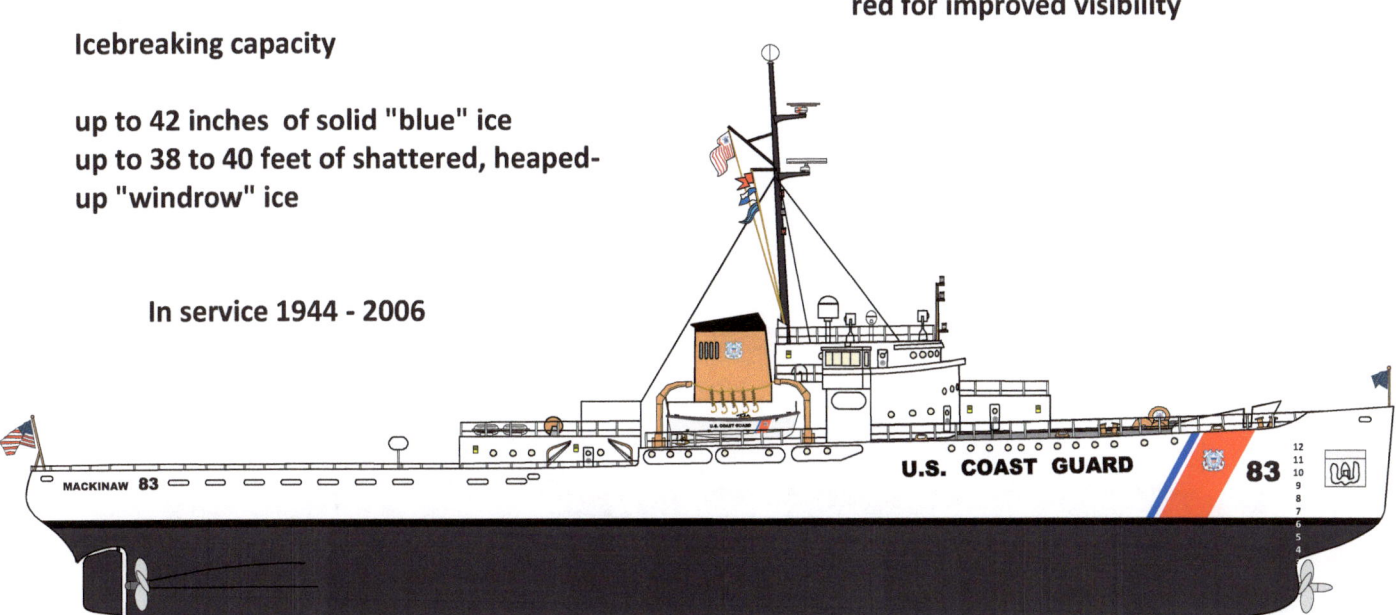

Displacement	5,252 long tons
Length	290 ft Beam 74.3 ft Draft 19.5 ft
Propulsion	6 × Fairbanks-Morse 10-cylinder Diesel engines, total 10,000 shp Three propellers
Speed	15 knots
Diesel fuel	276,000 U.S. gal
ballast water	345,828 U.S. gal
Complement	10 officers, 2 warrants, 132 enlisted (1945) 11 officers, 2 warrants, 122 enlisted (1965) 11 officers, 2 warrants, 64 enlisted (2005)

399 FOOT POLAR CLASS HEAVY ICEBREAKER (WAGB)

Builders	Lockheed Shipbuilding and Construction Company, Seattle, WA
Operators	United States Coast Guard
Built	1972–1978
Cost	50 million each
Completed	2

Icebreaking capacity

Up to 21 ft. thick
6 ft. at 3 knots

In service 1976 - Current

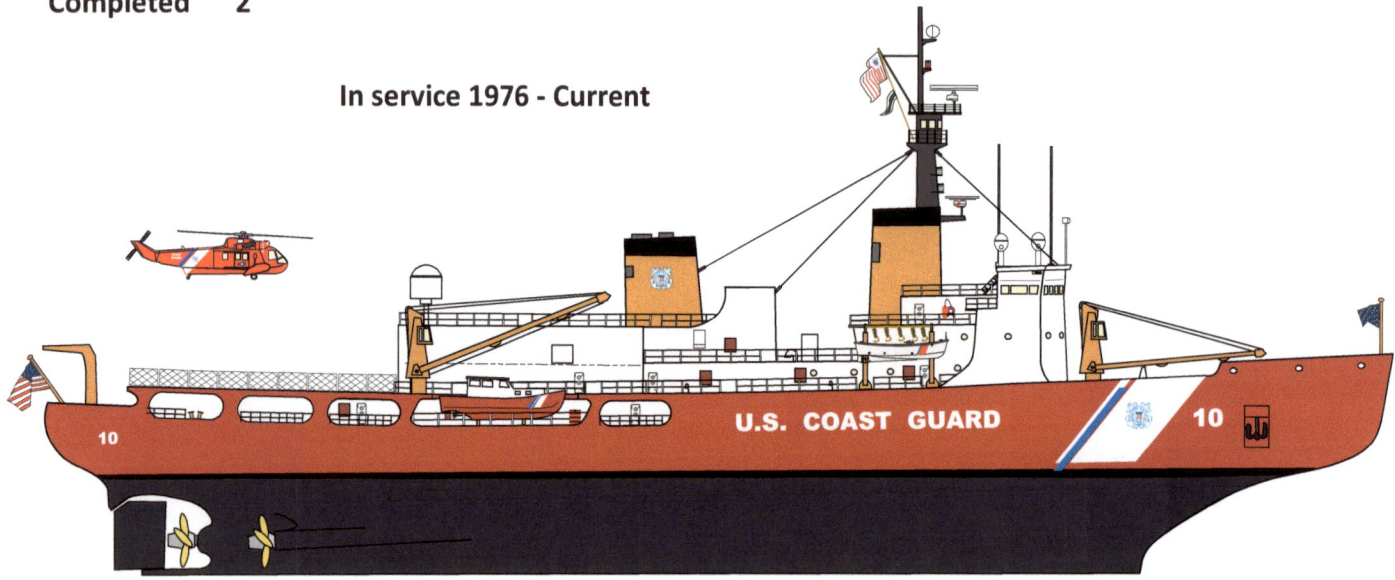

Displacement	10,863 long tons (standard) 13,623 long tons (full)
Length	399 ft Beam 83 ft 6 in Height 137 ft 10 in (from waterline) Draft 31 ft
Installed power	6 × Alco 16V-251F diesel engines 3,000 hp ea.
	3 × Pratt & Whitney FT-4A12 gas turbines 25,000 hp ea.
Propulsion	Combined diesel-electric or gas (CODLOG) 3 shafts; controllable pitch propellers
Speed	18 knots 3 knots in 6-foot ice
Range	16,000 nautical miles at 18 knots 28,275 nautical miles at 13 knots
Complement	15 officers 127 enlisted 33 scientists 12-person helicopter detachment
Aviation facilities	Helipad and hangar

420 FOOT MEDIUM ICEBREAKER HEALY (WAGB-20)

Builder	Avondale Shipyard Westwego, LA
Type	Medium Icebreaker
Vessels	built 1

Icebreaking capacity

3 knots in 4.5 ft ice. 10 ft thick when backing and ramming.

In service 1999 - Current

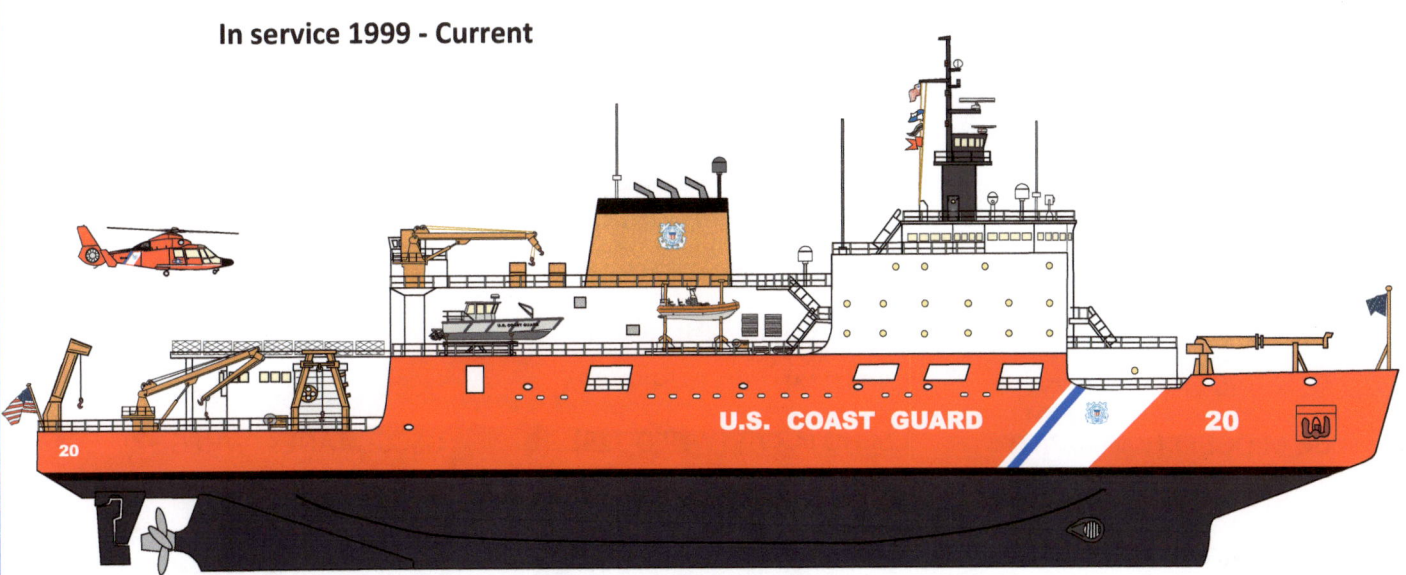

Displacement	16,000 long tons
Length	420 ft Beam 82 ft Draft 29 ft 3 in
Installed power	4 × Sulzer 12ZAV40S 46,350 hp (combined)
Propulsion	Diesel-electric Two shafts 15,000 hp
Speed	17 knots (maximum) 14 knots (cruising)
	Complement 19 officers 12 CPO 54 enlisted 51 scientists
Aircraft carried	2 × HH-65B Dolphin helicopters.
small boats carried	38 ft Arctic Survey Boat. 2 26 ft Cutter Boat Large (CBL)
Laboratories	Main Lab, Wet Lab, Bio-Chem Lab, Electronics Lab, Meteorological Lab

CUTTER AND ICEBREAKER NAMES

420' Healy Class Icebreaker (WAGB)

USCGC HEALY (WAGB-20)

418' Legend Class National Security Cutter, Large (WMSL)

USCGC BERTHOLF (WMSL-750)

USCGC WAESCHE (WMSL-751)

USCGC STRATTON (WMSL-752)

USCGC HAMILTON (WMSL-753)

USCGC JAMES (WMSL-754)

USCGC MUNRO (WMSL-755)

USCGC KIMBALL (WMSL-756)

USCGC MIDGETT (WMSL-757)

USCGC STONE (WMSL-758)

USCGC CALHOUN (WMSL-759)

399' Polar Class Icebreaker (WAGB)

USCGC POLAR STAR (WAGB-10)

USCGC POLAR SEA (WAGB-11)

378' High Endurance Cutter (WHEC)

USCGC HAMILTON (WHEC-715)

USCGC DALLAS (WHEC-716)

USCGC MELLON (WHEC-717)

USCGC CHASE (WHEC-718)

USCGC BOUTWELL (WHEC-719)

USCGC SHERMAN (WHEC-720)

USCGC GALLATIN (WHEC-721)

USCGC MORGENTHAU (WHEC-722)

USCGC RUSH (WHEC-723)

USCGC MUNRO (WHEC-724)

USCGC JARVIS (WHEC-725)

USCGC MIDGETT (WHEC-726)

360' Maritime Security Cutter, Medium (WMSM)

USCGC ARGUS (WMSM-915)

USCGC CHASE (WMSM-916)

USCGC INGHAM (WMSM-917)

USCGC RUSH (WMSM-918)

USCGC PICKERING (WMSM-919)

USCGC ICARUS (WMSM-920)

USCGC ACTIVE (WMSM-921)

USCGC DILIGENCE (WMSM-922)

USCGC ALERT (WMSM-923)

USCGC VIGILANT (WMSM-924)

USCGC RELIANCE (WMSM-925)

327' Treasury Class Cutter (WHEC)

USCGC BIBB (WHEC 31)

USCGC CAMPBELL (WHEC 32)

USCGC DUANE (WHEC 33)

USCGC HAMILTON (WHEC 34)

USCGC INGHAM (WHEC 35)

USCGC SPENCER (WHEC 36)

USCGC TANEY (WHEC 37)

CUTTER AND ICEBREAKER NAMES

311' Casco Class Cutter (WHEC)

CASCO (WHEC-370)
MATAGORDA (WHEC-373)
HUMBOLDT (WHEC-372)
MACKINAC (WHEC-371)
ABSECON (WHEC-374)
CHINCOTEAGUE (WHEC-375)
COOS BAY (WHEC-376)
ROCKAWAY (WHEC-377)
HALF MOON (WHEC-378)
UNIMAK (WHEC-379)
YAKUTAT (WHEC-380)
BARATARIA (WHEC-381)
BERING STRAIT (WHEC-382)
CASTLE ROCK (WHEC-383),
COOK INLET (WHEC-384)
DEXTER (WHEC-385)
MCCULLOCH (WHEC-386)
GRESHAM (WHEC-387)

309' Icebreaker (WAGB)

USCGC GLACIER (WAGB-4)

290' Medium Great Lakes Icebreaker (WAGB)

USCGC MACKINAW (WAGB-83)

282' Medium Endurance Cutter (WMEC)

USCGC ALEX HALEY (WMEC-39)

270' Medium Endurance Cutter (WMEC)

USCGC BEAR (WMEC-901)
USCGC TAMPA (WMEC-902)
USCGC HARRIET LANE (WMEC-903)
USCGC NORTHLAND (WMEC-904)
USCGC SPENCER (WMEC-905)
USCGC SENECA (WMEC-906)
USCGC ESCANABA (WMEC-907)
USCGC TAHOMA (WMEC-908)
USCGC CAMPBELL (WMEC-909)
USCGC THETIS (WMEC-910)
USCGC FORWARD (WMEC-911)
USCGC LEGARE (WMEC-912)
USCGC MOHAWK (WMEC-913)

269' Wind Class Icebreaker (WAGB)

USCGC STATEN ISLAND (WAGB-278)
USCGC EASTWIND (WAGB-279)
USCGC SOUTHWIND (WAGB-280)
USCGC WESTWIND (WAGB 281)
USCGC NORTHWIND (WAGB-282)
USCGC BURTON ISLAND (WAGB-283)
USCGC EDISTO (WAGB-284)

255' Owasco Class Cutter (WHEC)

USCGC OWASCO (WHEC-39)
USCGC WINNEBAGO (WHEC-40)
USCGC CHAUTAUQUA (WHEC-41)
USCGC SEBAGO (WHEC-42)
USCGC IROQUOIS (WHEC-43)
USCGC WACHUSETT (WHEC-44)
USCGC ESCANABA (WHEC-64)
USCGC WINONA (WHEC-65)
USCGC KLAMATH (WHEC-66)
USCGC MINNETONKA (WHEC-67)
USCGC ANDROSCOGGIN (WHEC-68)
USCGC MENDOTA (WHEC-69)
USCGC PONTCHARTRAIN (WHEC-70)

240' Seagoing Buoy Tender Breaker (WLBB)

USCGC MACKINAW (WLBB-30)

230' Medium Endurance Cutter (WMEC)

USCGC STORIS (WMEC-38)

CUTTER, ICEBREAKER AND TUG NAMES

213' Medium Endurance Cutter (WMEC)
USCGC ACUSHNET (WMEC-167)
USCGC YOCONA (WMEC-168)
USCGC ESCAPE (WMEC-6)

210' Medium Endurance Cutter (WMEC)
USCGC RELIANCE (WMEC-615)
USCGC DILIGENCE (WMEC-616)
USCGC VIGILANT (WMEC-617)
USCGC ACTIVE (WMEC-618)
USCGC CONFIDENCE (WMEC-619)
USCGC RESOLUTE (WMEC-620)
USCGC VALIANT (WMEC-621)
USCGC COURAGEOUS (WMEC-622)
USCGC STEADFAST (WMEC-623)
USCGC DAUNTLESS (WMEC-624)
USCGC VENTUROUS (WMEC-625)
USCGC DEPENDABLE (WMEC-626)
USCGC VIGOROUS (WMEC-627)
USCGC DURABLE (WMEC-628)
USCGC DECISIVE (WMEC-629)
USCGC ALERT (WMEC-630)

205' Cherokee/Navajo Class Tug (WMEC)
USCGC UTE (WMEC-76)
USCGC LIPAN (WMEC-85)
USCGC AVOYEL (WMEC-150)
USCGC CHILULA (WMEC-153)
USCGC CHEROKEE (WMEC-165)
USCGC TAMAROA (WMEC-166)

180 ft Medium Endurance Cutter
USCGC EVERGREEN (WAGO-295)
USCG CITRIS (WMEC)

143' Auxiliary Tug (WMEC)
USCGC MODOC (WMEC-194)
USCGC COMANCHE (WMEC-202)

140' Bay Class Icebreaking Tug (WTGB)
USCGC KATMAI BAY (WTGB-101)
USCGC BRISTOL BAY (WTGB-102)
USCGC MOBILE BAY (WTGB-103)
USCGC BISCAYNE BAY (WTGB-104)
USCGC NEAH BAY (WTGB-105)
USCGC MORRO BAY (WTGB-106)
USCGC PENOBSCOT BAY (WTGB-107)
USCGC THUNDER BAY (WTGB-108)
USCGC STURGEON BAY (WTGB-109)

125' Active Class Patrol Boat (WPB)
USCGC ACTIVE (WPB-125)
USCGC AGASSIZ (WPB-126)
USCGC ALERT (WPB-127)
USCGC BEDLOE (WPB-128)
USCGC BONHAM (WPB-129)
USCGC BOUTWELL (WPB-130)
USCGC CAHOONE (WPB-131)
USCGC CARTIGAN (WPB-132)
USCGC COLFAX (WPB-133)
USCGC CRAWFORD (WPB-134)
USCGC DILIGENCE (WPB-135)
USCGC DIX (WPB-136)
USCGC EWING (WPB-137)
USCGC FAUNCE (WPB-138)
USCGC FREDERICK LEE (WPB-139)
USCGC GENERAL GREENE (WPC-140)
USCGC HARRIET LANE (WPB-141)
USCGC JACKSON (WPB-142)
USCGC KIMBALL (WPB-143)
USCGC LEGARE (WPB-144)
USCGC MARION (WPB-145)

CUTTER, ICEBREAKER AND TUG NAMES

125' Active Class Patrol Boat (WMEC)
USCGC MCLANE (WMEC-146)
USCGC MORRIS (WSC-147)
USCGC NEMAHA (WMEC-148)
USCGC PULASKI (WMEC-149)
USCGC RELIANCE (WMEC-150)
USCGC RUSH (WMEC-151)
USCGC TIGER (WMEC-152)
USCGC TRAVIS (WMEC-153)
USCGC VIGILANT (WMEC-154)
USCGC WOODBURY (WMEC-155)
USCGC YEATON (WMEC-156)
USCGC CUYAHOGA (WIX-157)

110' Arundel Class Harbor Tug (WYTM/WYT)
USCGC ARUNDEL (WYT-90)
USCGC MAHONING (WYT-91)
USCGC NAUGHATUCK (WYT-92)
USCGC RARITAN (WYT-93)

110' Manitou Class Harbor Tug (WYTM/WYT)
USCGC MANITOU (WYTM-60)
USCGC KAW (WYTM-61)

110' Apalachee Class Harbor Tug (WYT)
USCGC APALACHEE (WYT-71)
USCGC YANKTON (WYT-72)
USCGC MOHICAN (WYT-73)
USCGC CHINOOK (WYTM-96)
USCGC OJIBWA (WYT-97)
USCGC SNOHOMISH (WYT-98)
USCGC SAUK (WYT-99)

85' ST Class Harbor Tug (WYT)
USCGC MESSENGER (WYT-85009)
USCGC RESEARCH (WYT-850010)

65' Small Harbor Tug (WYTL)
USCGC CAPSTAN (WYTL-65601)
USCGC CHOCK (WYTL-65602)
USCGC SWIVEL (WYTL-65603)
USCGC TACKLE (WYTL-65604)
USCGC TOWLINE (WYTL-65605)
USCGC CATENARY (WYTL-65606)
USCGC BRIDLE (WYTL-65607)
USCGC PENDANT (WYTL-65608)
USCGC SHACKLE (WYTL-65609)
USCGC HAWSER (WYTL-65610)
USCGC LINE (WYTL-65611)
USCGC WIRE (WYTL-65612)
USCGC BITT (WYTL-65613)
USCGC BOLLARD (WYTL-65614)
USCGC CLEAT (WYTL-65615)

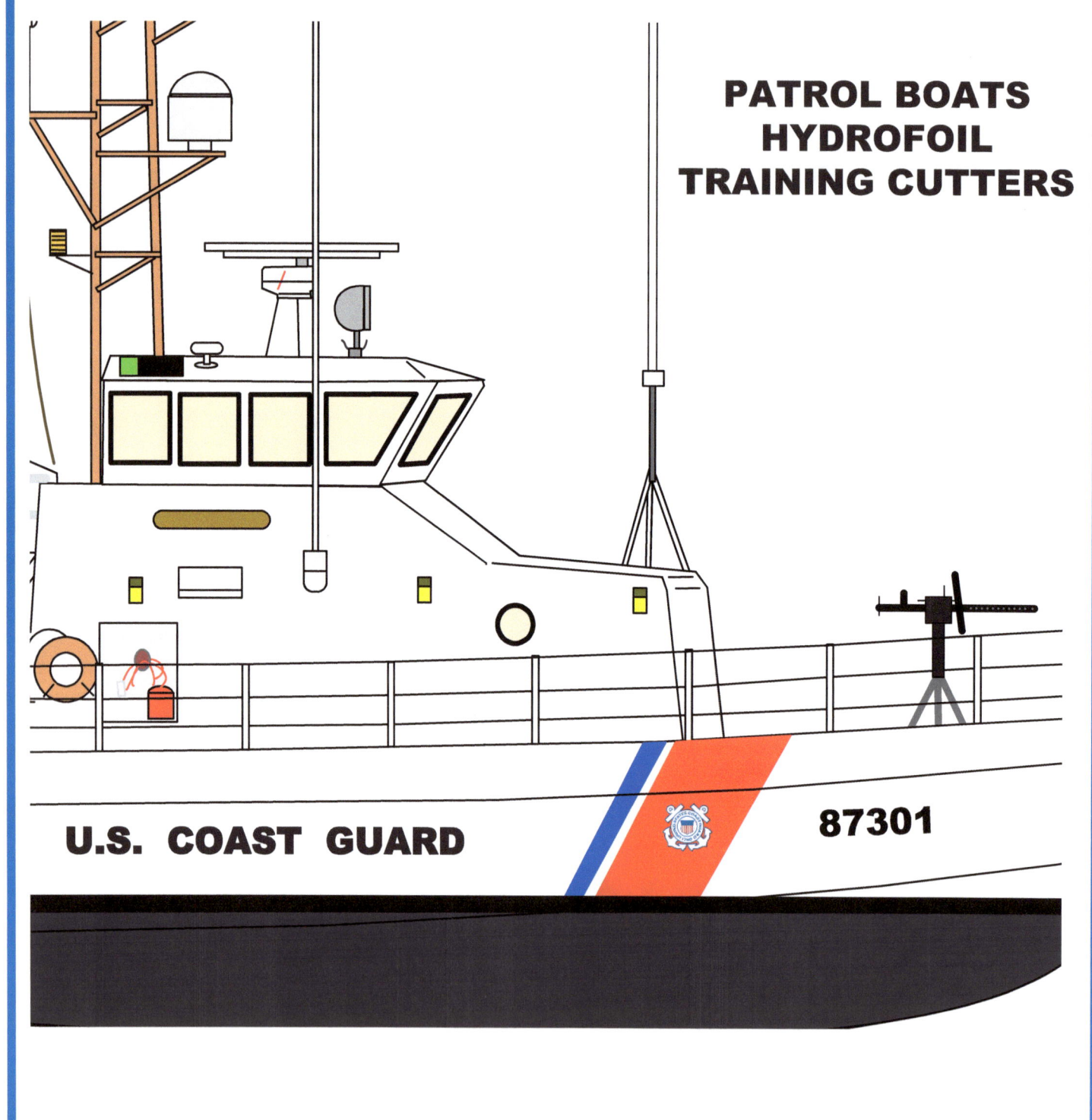

WPB	Patrol boat
WPC	Patrol cutter (referred to as fast response cutters)
WSES	Surface effect ship
WPBH	Hydrofoil

Patrol boats operate in coastal waters and conduct search and rescue operations and law enforcement patrols. 26 of the Point-class cutters were transported to Vietnam to serve with Coast Guard crews under U.S. Navy control. All 26 remained in Vietnam and did not return to the U.S. The hydrofoil Flagstaff was loaned to the Coast Guard by the Navy for testing, and she continually suffered mechanical breakdowns and proved to be very costly to operate. Eight of the Island class boats received a hull extension to 123 feet but suffered hull cracks and were immediately taken out of service.

| WIX | Training cutter |

Several cutters served or still serve as training platforms with the most famous being the bark Eagle. The Eagle sails on cruises from ranging from a week to two months with Academy students and candidates from the Officer Candidate School. The Cuyahoga, was homeported at the Reserve Training Center at Yorktown, VA and trained officer candidates. The Courier was homeported at the Reserve Training Center in Yorktown, and she served as a training vessel for reservists.

73 FOOT USCGC FLAGSTAFF (WPBH 1)

Commissioned 14 September 1968 (USN);
8 November 1974 to 2 March 1977 on loan from USN
Type   Hydrofoil gunboat

In service 1974 - 1977

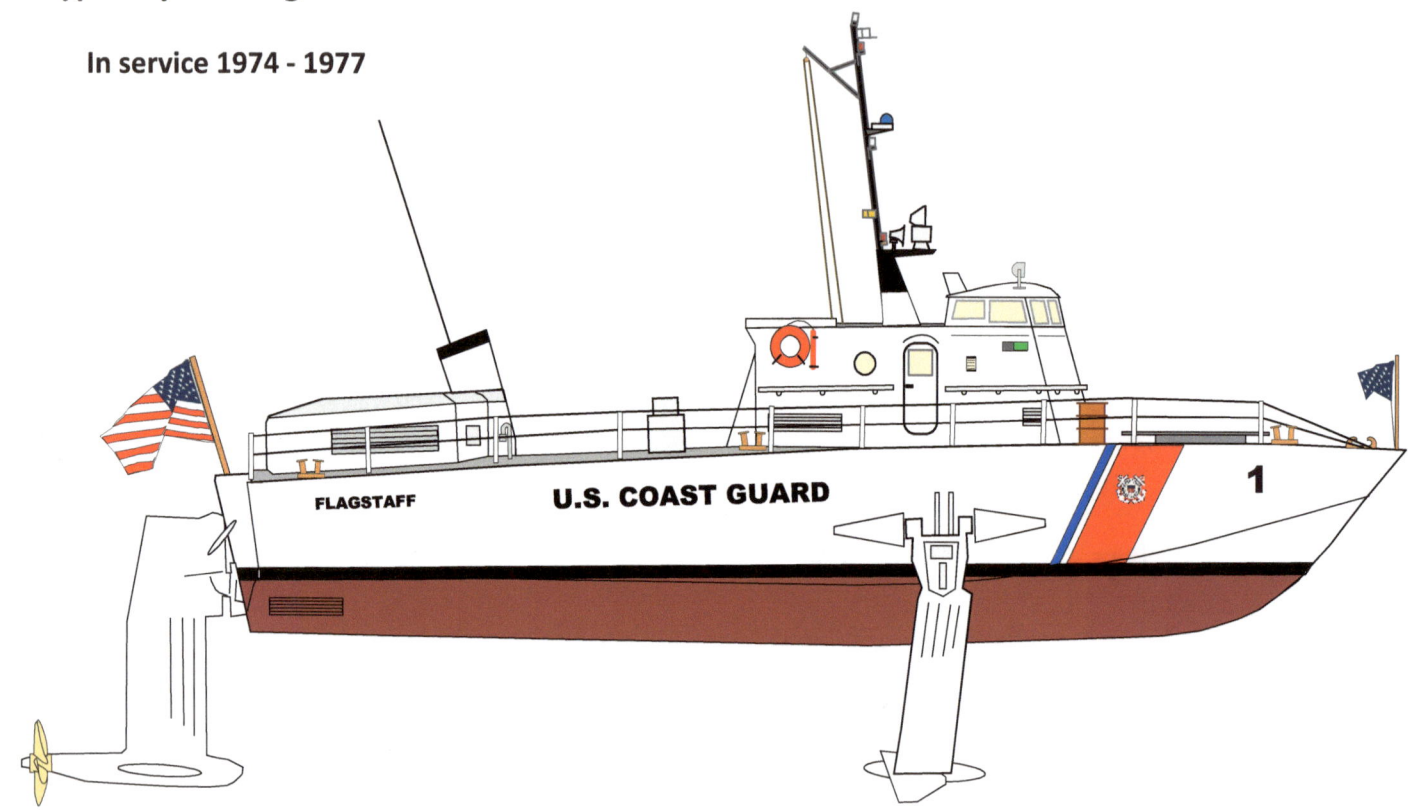

Displacement	67 long tons
Length	82 ft length overall Beam 21 ft 6 in Draft 4 ft 4 in 18 ft (foils extended)
Propulsion	Rolls-Royce Tyne gas turbine with supercavitating propeller (foil-borne)
	2 × General Motors diesel engines with water-jet pumps (hull-borne)
Speed	Max: at least 45 kn (foil-borne)
Complement	12 (1974); 13 (1977)
Armament	1 × 40 mm Bofors AA gun, 1 × 81 mm (3.2 in) mortar, 2 × .50 in (12.7 mm) M2 Browning machine gun

82 FOOT POINT CLASS PATROL BOAT (WPB)

82301 to 82344, 82371 to 83379   built at USCG yard Curtis Bay MD.
82345 to 82370   built at J.M. Martinac Tacoma, WA

Built   79   1960–1970

In service 1960 - 2003

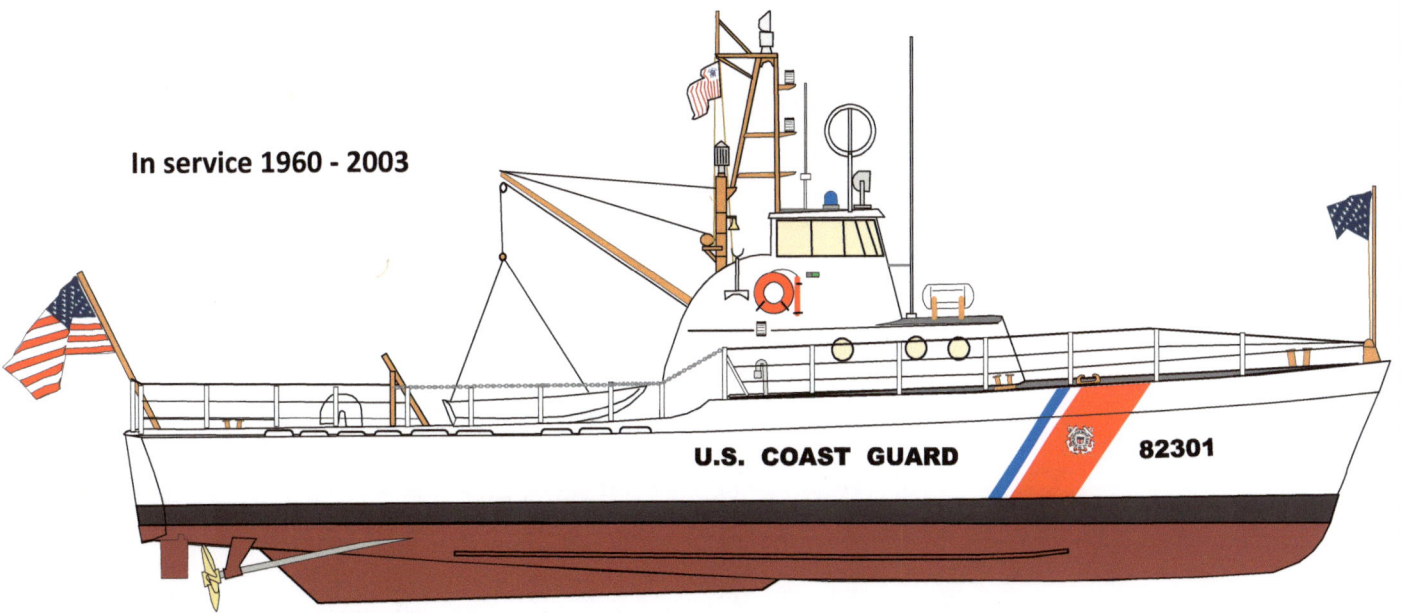

Displacement:	60–69 tons
Length:	82 ft 10 in Beam: 17 ft 7 in max Draft: 5 ft 11 in
Propulsion:	(2) 600 hp Cummins diesel, (2) 800 hp Cummins diesel
	(2) 1,000 hp gas turbine, hull 82314
Speed:	16.8 kn
Range:	577 miles at 14.5 knots 1271 miles at 10.7 knots
Complement:	domestic service, 8 men; (Vietnam service, 2 officers, 8 men)
Armament	1960- 1 × Oerlikon 20 mm cannon
	Vietnam service 5 × M2 Browning machine guns 1 × 81 mm M29 mortar

82 FOOT POINT CLASS PATROL BOAT (WPB) SQUADRON ONE

Complement Vietnam service, 2 officers, 8 men
Armament 1 × Oerlikon 20 mm cannon
Vietnam service 5 × M2 Browning machine guns 1 × 81 mm M29 mortar

Coast Guard Squadron One

Decorations Presidential Unit Citation Navy
Navy Unit Commendation
Meritorious Unit Commendation Navy

Engagements Vietnam War
Operation Market Time
Operation Sealords

In service, USCG squadron one
1965 - 1970

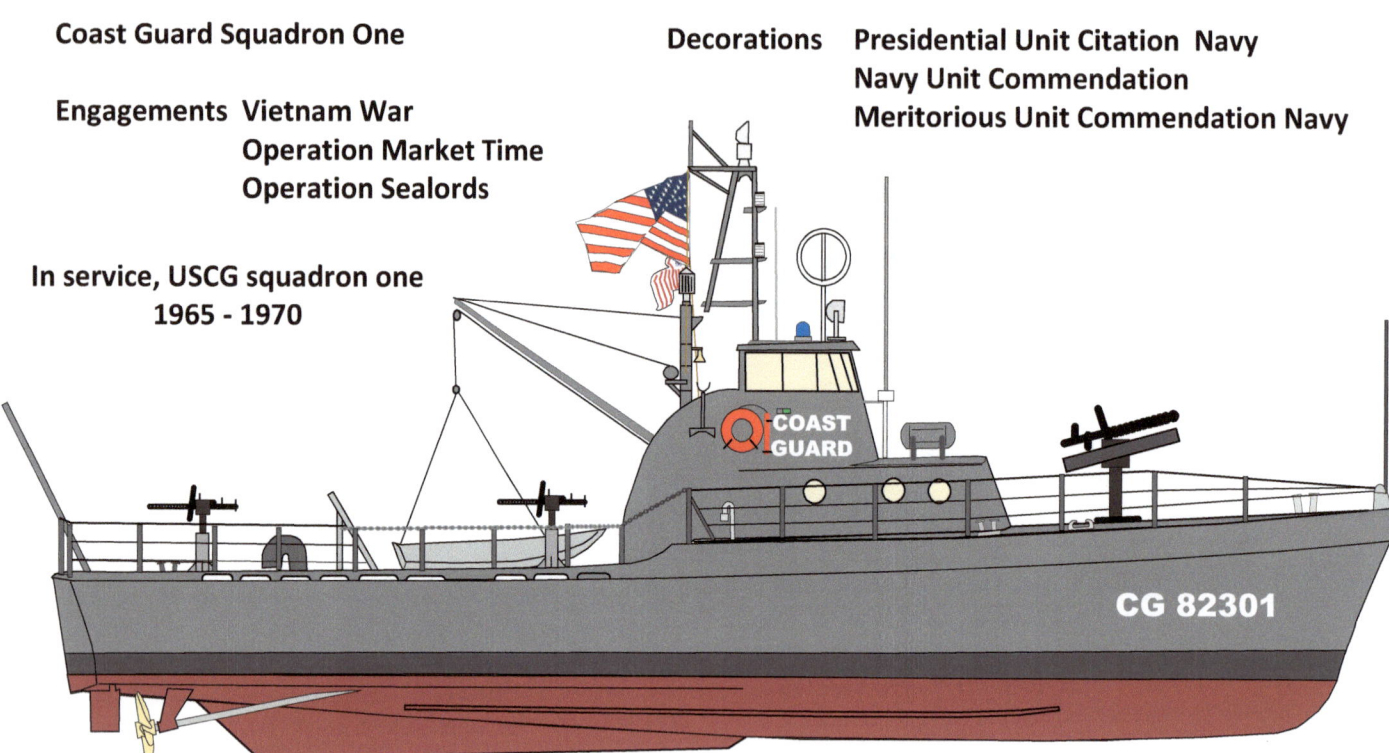

Point Caution	WPB-82301	Point Slocum	WPB-82313	Point Grey	WPB-82324
Point Young	WPB-82303	Point Clear	WPB-82315	Point Dume	WPB-82325
Point League	WPB-82304	Point Mast	WPB-82316	Point Cypress	WPB-82326
Point Partridge	WPB-82305	Point Comfort	WPB-82317	Point Banks	WPB-82327
Point Jefferson	WPB-82306	Point Orient	WPB-82319	Point Gammon	WPB-82328
Point Glover	WPB-82307	Point Kennedy	WPB-82320	Point Welcome	WPB-82329
Point White	WPB-82308	Point Lomas	WPB-82321	Point Ellis	WPB-82330
Point Arden	WPB-82309	Point Hudson	WPB-82322		
Point Garnet	WPB-82310	Point Grace	WPB-82323		

87 FOOT MARINE PROTECTOR CLASS PATROL BOAT (WPB)

Builder: Bollinger Shipyards, Lockport, La
Completed: 73
Numbers: 87301 – 87374
Cost: 5 million

Sea Devil and Sea Fox are assigned to the United States Navy submarine base in Kings Bay, Georgia.

In service 1998 - Current

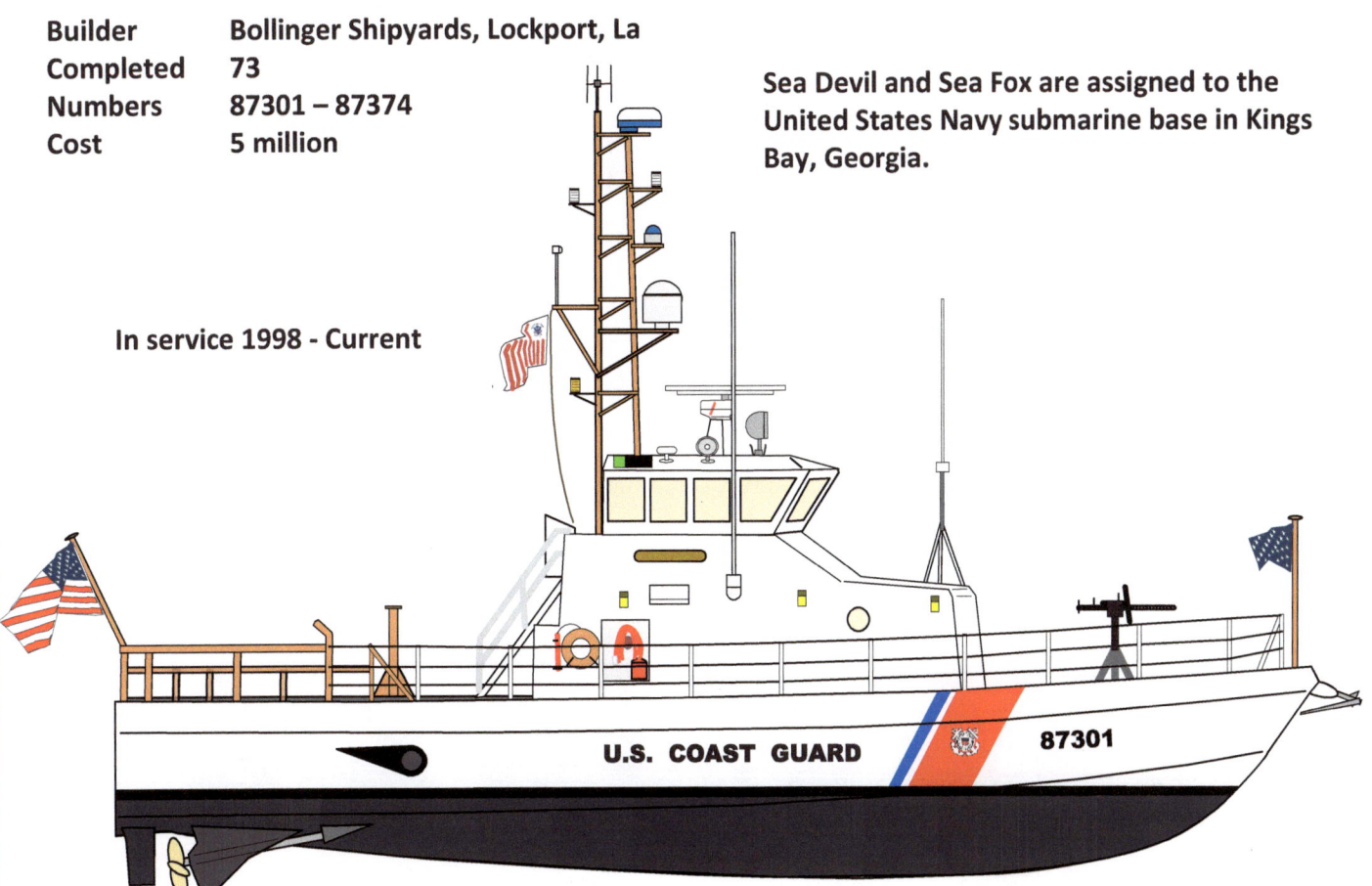

Displacement: 100 tons
Length: 87 ft Beam 19 ft 5 in Draft 5 ft 7 in
Propulsion: 2 x MTU diesels
Speed: 25 knots
Range: 612 nm
Endurance: 3 days
Complement: 11
Sensors: 1 x AN/SPS-73 surface search radar
Armament: 2 × .50 caliber M2 Browning machine guns

95 FOOT CAPE CLASS PATROL BOAT (WPB)

Builder	Coast Guard Yard Curtis Bay, Baltimore MD.
Numbered	95300 – 95335
Built	36

Type A was outfitted for ASW
Type B was outfitted for search and rescue
Type C built with a deck house aft of the bridge

In service 1953 - 1990

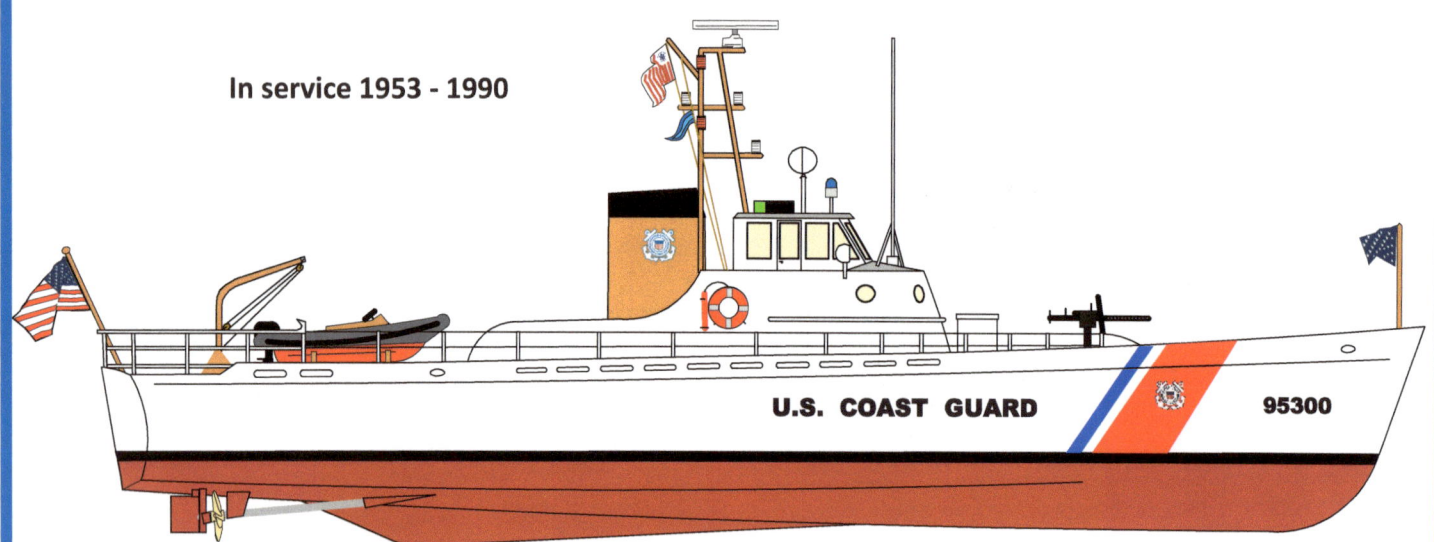

Displacement	105 tons fully loaded
Length	95 ft Beam 20 ft max Draft 6 ft 5 in
Propulsion	4 Cummins VT-600 diesels , 2200 hp
	after renovation 2 Detroit 16V149 diesels, 2470 hp
Speed	22 knots max, renovated, 24 knots
Range	1,700 mi at 12 knots
Complement	15
Armament	2 mousetrap depth charge racks, 2 20mm twin Oerlikon cannons, 2 .50 cal machine guns, 2 40mm Mk 19 grenade launchers

110 FOOT ISLAND CLASS PATROL BOAT (WPB)

Builder	Bollinger Shipyards, Lockport, La
hull numbers	WPB-1301 - WPB-1349
Built	49 1985–1992
Cost	7,000,000 each

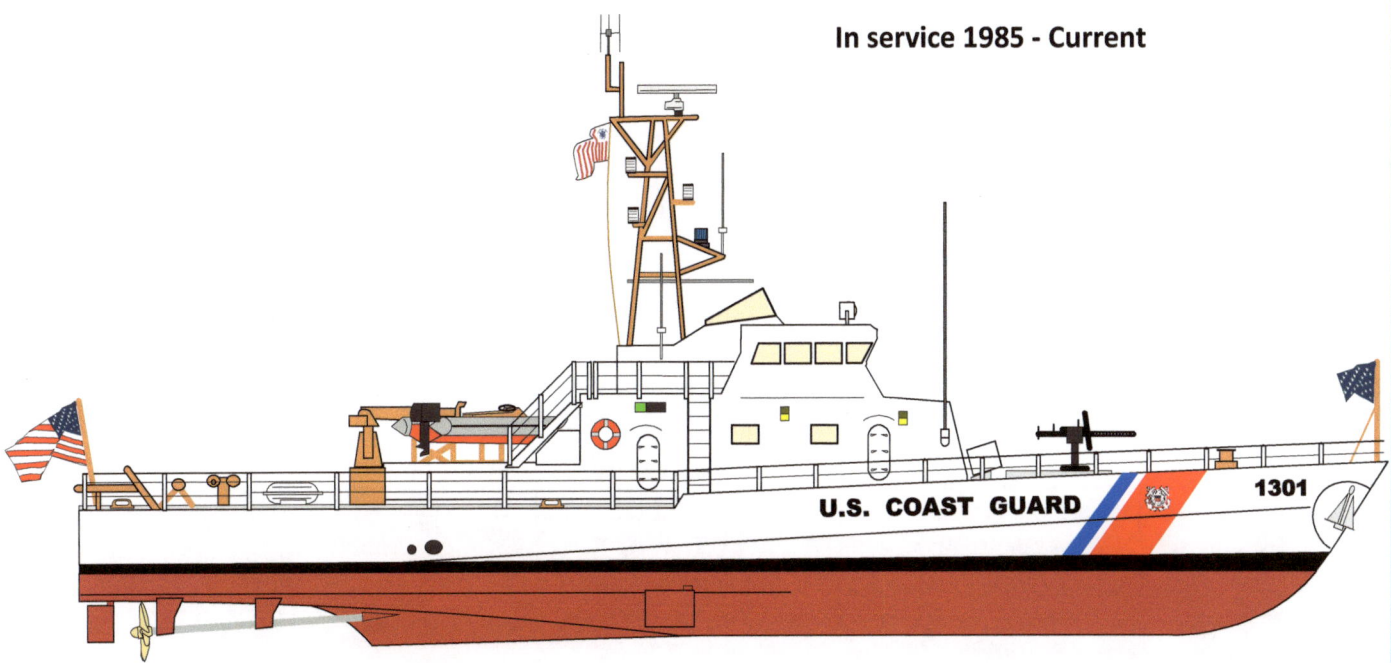

In service 1985 - Current

Displacement	165 tons
Length	110 ft Beam 21 ft Draft 7.3 ft
Propulsion	2x Paxman Valenta V16 – 16RP200[2] or
	2x Caterpillar diesel engines
Speed	29.5 knots Range 3,300 nm Endurance 5 days
Boats carried	1 – Cutter Boat Medium
Complement	17 (2 officers, 15 enlisted)
Sensors and processing systems	AN/SPS-73 radar
Armament	Mk 38 25 mm chain gun
	2 × M2 .50-cal MG

110 FOOT SEABIRD CLASS SURFACE EFFECT SHIP (WSES)

Dorado-Class Surface-Effect Ships
Builder   Bell Halter Inc., New Orleans, La
Cost: $5,000,000 1982

Dorado   (WSES-1)
Sea Hawk   (WSES-2)
Shearwater   (WSES-3)
Petrel   (WSES-4)

In service 1981 - 1994

Displacement 152 long tons
Length: 109' 1" Beam: 39' Draft: 9' 7" (full load); 6' (on cushion)
Main Engines 2 Detroit 16V149TIB Diesel engines (1,800 hp @ 1,900 rpm)
Lift Engines: 2 Detroit 8V92 Diesel engines (378 hp @ 2,000 rpm)
Performance   Max: 30+ knots Cruising: 25 knots
Range   1,100 mile
Complement: 17
Armament: Small arms

123 Foot Island Class Patrol Boat (WPB)

In 2002 as part of the Integrated Deepwater System Program, Bollinger Shipyards refitted 8 Island class cutters including adding 13 feet to the stern for a high-speed stern launching ramp, new superstructure that made room to accommodate mixed-gender crews.

In service 2004 - 2006

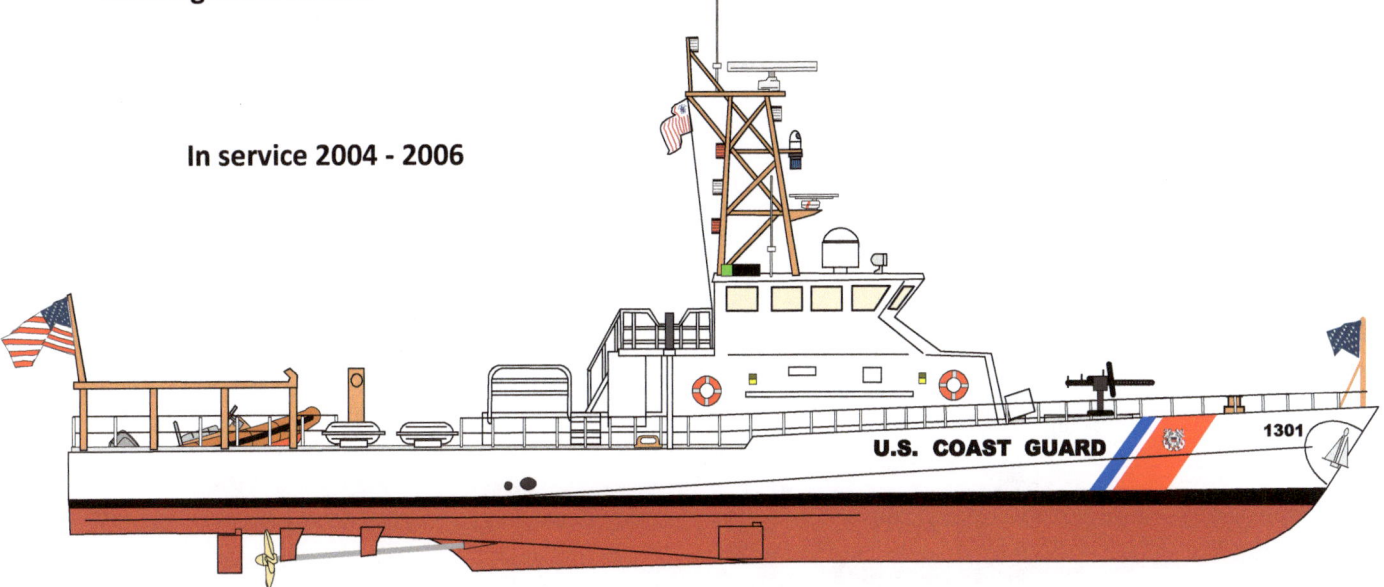

November 2006 all eight of the 123 ft WPBs were taken out of service due hulls cracking when driven at high speed or in rough weather.

  Displacement 183 tons
  Length   123 ft Beam 21 ft Draft 7.3 ft
  Propulsion 2x Paxman Valenta V16 – 16RP200[2] or
         2x Caterpillar diesel engines
  Speed   28.5 kn Range 2,900 nm Endurance 5 days
  Boats carried 1 – Cutter Boat Medium stern launch
  Complement 16 (2 officers, 14 enlisted)
  Sensors   AN/SPS-73 radar
  Armament Mk 38 25 mm chain gun
         2 × M2 .50-cal MG

154 FOOT SENTINEL CLASS (WPC)

Also known as the Fast Response Cutter

Builder   Bollinger Shipyards Lockport, La
Completed   65
Cost $3.8 billion total contract
Numbered   1101 -1166

In service 2012 - Current

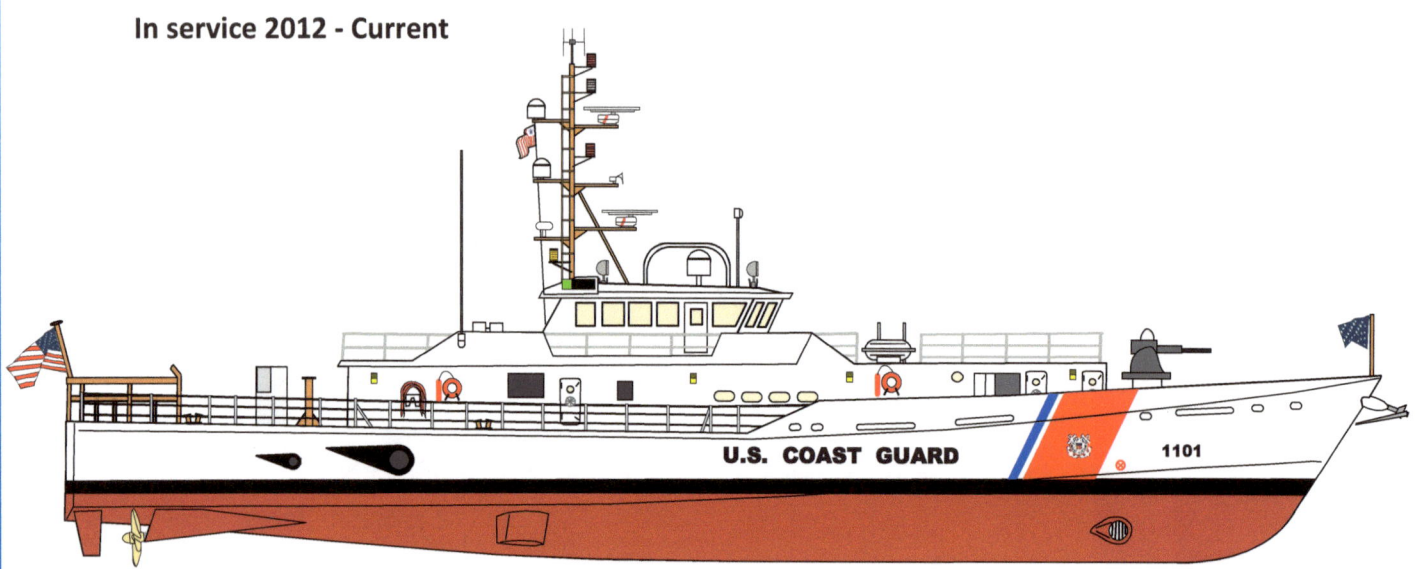

Displacement   353 long tons
Length   154 ft Beam 25.6 ft Depth 8 ft
Propulsion   2 × 5,800 shp MTU diesel engines
                1 × 101 shp bow thruster
Speed   28+ knots
Endurance   5 days, 2,500 nautical miles
craft carried   1 × Cutter Boat – Over the Horizon – Jet-drive
Complement   4 officers, 20 crew
Armament   1 × Mk 38 Mod 2 25 mm Machine Gun System
               4 × crew-served Browning M2 machine guns

179 FOOT CYCLONE CLASS PATROL BOAT (WPC)

Built for the United States Naval Special Warfare Command
Builder Bollinger Shipyards
Planned 16
Completed 14

6 loaned to the Coast Guard between 2000 to 2004

Displacement	328.5 long tons
Length	179 ft Beam 25 ft Draft 7.5 ft
Propulsion	4 × Paxman 16RP200- 1-CM diesel engines 3,350 shp
	4 × shafts, Reintjes reverse reduction gear box
Speed	35 knots
Range	2,000–2,500 nmi at 12 kn
Crew	4 officers, 24 enlisted personnel
Armament	2 × 25 mm MK 38 autocannon
	2 × .50 in caliber machine guns
	2 × 40 mm MK 19 automatic grenade launchers
	2 × 7.62 mm M240B machine guns
	6 × FIM-92 Stinger SAMs
	2 × MK-60 quadruple BGM-176B Griffin B missile launchers

125 FOOT ACTIVE CLASS PATROL BOAT (WIX)

Builder	American Brown Boveri Electric Corporation, Camden, Nj
Cost	$63,173 (1927)
Built	1926–1927
Completed	35
Numbered	125 to 157

WIX-157 Cuyhoga
Queen of the fleet status

In service 1927 - 1978

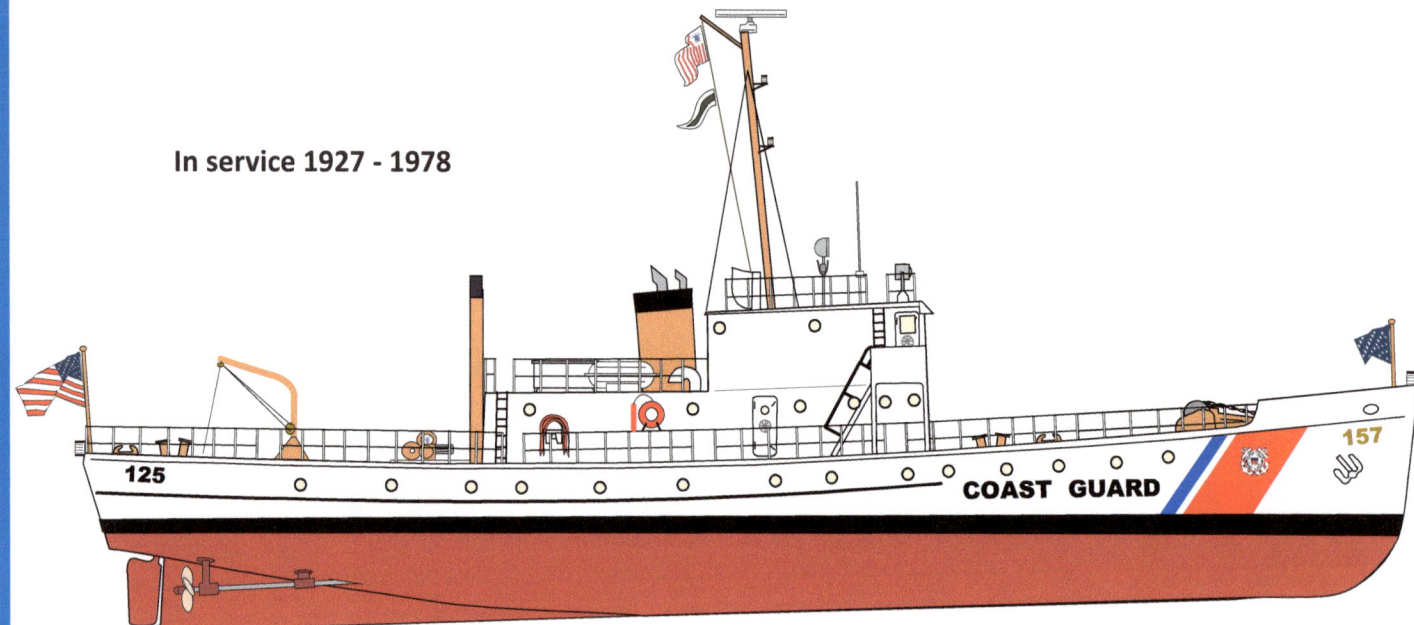

Displacement	232 long tons
Length	125 ft Beam 23 ft 6 in Draft 7 ft 6 in
Propulsion	At launch: 2 × 6-cylinder, 300 hp Winton Model 114-6 diesel engines
	1938: 2 x Cooper-Bessemer EN-9 600 bhp diesel engines
Speed Maximum	13 knots Cruise: 8 kn
Range	3,500 nm at max. speed: 2,500 nmi
Complement	1938: 22 1944: 38 1960: 3 officers, 17 men
Armament	1927: 1 × 3"/27 caliber gun
	1941: 1 × 3"/23 caliber gun 2 × depth charge tracks, 10 depth charges
	1945: 1 × 40 mm/60 (single) 2 × 20 mm/70 (single) 2 × depth charge tracks
	2 × Mousetrap ASW
	1960: 1 × 40 mm/60

180 FOOT CACTUS CLASS TRAINING CUTTER (WIX)

Class A or Cactus-class seagoing buoy tenders

Builder   Zenith Dredge Company, Duluth, Minnesota 1941
Cost $925,464
Number   290

In service as WLB   1942 - 1998

In service as WIX   1999 - 2006

GENTIAN's career as a buoy tender ended in May 1998. Under her new designation as a Caribbean Support Tender (WIX-290), GENTIAN operated with a multinational crew including twenty-nine U.S. personnel and sixteen representatives from Caribbean navies and coast guards. The tender also delivers various cargos from the United States to the Caribbean and functions as a floating workshop.

Displacement 1,025 tons
Length 180 ft Beam 37 ft Draft 12 ft
Propulsion   2 × General Motors EMD 645 V8 diesel engines
Speed 8.3 kn cruising 13 kn maximum
Range 8,000 nm at 13 kn
Complement   3 officers, 2 warrant officers, 42 enlisted
Armament Wartime 1 × 3 in (76 mm) gun 20 mm guns Depth charges

295 FOOT GORCH FOCK CLASS BARQUE (WIX-327)

Builder	Blohm & Voss, Hamburg	Captured	April 1945
Launched	13 June 1936	Transferred to the United States	
		Homeport	U.S. Coast Guard Academy
			New London, Ct

In service 1946 - Current

Displacement	1,816 tons
Length	295 ft Beam 39 ft Draft Full load: 17 ft
Installed power	2 × 430 hp Caterpillar 3406 generators
Propulsion	1 × 1,200 hp MTU 8V 4000 diesel engine
Sail plan Foremast	147.3 ft Mainmast: 147.3 ft Mizzenmast: 132.0 ft Sail area: 22,280 sq ft
Speed	Sail 19 knots Diesel: 10 knots
Range Sail	Unlimited Diesel: 5,450 nmi at 7.5 kn
Complement	Permanent: 6 officers, 54 crew

338 FOOT CLASS C1-M-AV1 (WAGR-WTR)

USCGC Kukui (WAK-186) length 388 ft 8 in supplied the equipment and personnel for the construction and logistical support of the Pacific Loran-A and Loran-C systems

USCGC Courier (WAGR-410) Length 338 ft mobile transmitting facility for the U.S. Information Agency's "Voice of America" program, mobile operational training platform, training vessel for reservists. She carried accommodations for 220 trainees, patrol boats, and communication equipment

Builder	Froemming Brothers, Milwaukee, WI.
Launched	1945
Commissioned	25 March 1945
Commissioned	USCG 15 February 1952 (USCG WAGR-410)

In service 1945 - 1972

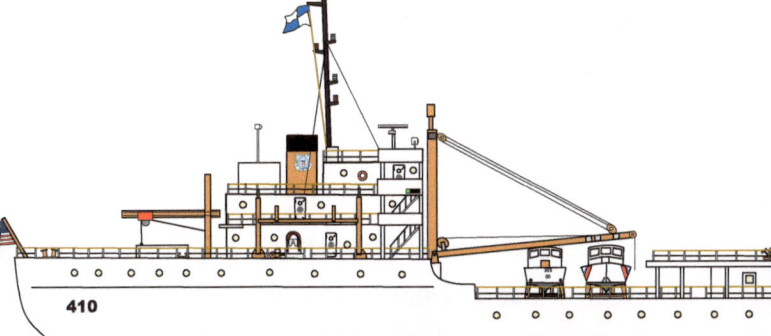

Displacement	5,650 long tons
Length	338.75 ft Beam 50.33 ft Draft 17.25 ft
Propulsion	1 × 1,700 SHP two-cycle 6-cylinder Norberg diesel; single screw
Speed	10.6 kn maximum
Range	24,273 miles
Complement	10 officers, 45 enlisted. 3 radio engineers, 1 program coordinator.
Communications	radio transmitter RCA BT-105 150-kilowatt two Collins 207B1 type 35-kilowatt Collins Radio Company 51J-type receiver

PATROL BOATS AND TRAINING CUTTERS

338' C1-M-AVI (WTR-WIX)

USCGC COURIER

295' Training Barque Eagle (WIX)

USCGC EAGLE (WIX-327)

180' Cactus-class support tender (WIX)

USCGC GENTIAN (WIX-290)

179' Patrol Coastal (WPC)

USCGC TEMPEST (WPC-2)

USCGC MONSOON (WPC-4)

USCGC ZEPHYR (WPC-8)

USCGC SHAMAL (WPC-13)

USCGC TORNADO (WPC-14)

154' Sentinel Class Fast Response Cutter (WPC)

USCGC BERNARD C. WEBBER (WPC-1101)

USCGC RICHARD ETHERIDGE (WPC-1102)

USCGC WILLIAM FLORES (WPC-1103)

USCGC ROBERT YERED (WPC-1104)

USCGC MARGARET NORVELL (WPC-1105)

USCGC PAUL CLARK (WPC-1106)

USCGC CHARLES DAVID (WPC-1107)

USCGC CHARLES W. SEXTON (WPC-1108)

USCGC KATHLEEN MOORE (WPC-1109)

USCGC RAYMOND EVANS (WPC-1110)

USCGC WILLIAM TRUMP (WPC-1111)

USCGC ISAAC MAYO (WPC-1112)

USCGC RICHARD DIXON (WPC-1113)

USCGC HERIBERTO HERNANDEZ (WPC-1114)

USCGC JOSEPH NAPIER (WPC-1115)

USCGC WINSLOW W. GRIESSER (WPC-1116)

USCGC DONALD HORSLEY (WPC-1117)

USCGC JOSEPH TEZANOS (WPC-1118)

USCGC ROLLIN A. FRITCH (WPC-1119)

USCGC LAWRENCE O. LAWSON (WPC-1120)

USCGC JOHN F. MCCORMICK (WPC-1121)

USCGC BAILEY T. BARCO (WPC-1122)

USCGC BENJAMIN B. DAILEY (WPC-1123)

USCGC OLIVER F. BERRY (WPC-1124)

USCGC JACOB POROO (WPC-1125)

USCGC JOSEPH GERCZAK (WPC-1126)

USCGC RICHARD SNYDER (WPC-1127)

USCGC NATHAN BRUCKENTHAL (WPC-1128)

USCGC FORREST REDNOUR (WPC-1129)

USCGC ROBERT WARD (WPC-1130)

USCGC TERRELL HORNE (WPC-1131)

USCGC BENJAMIN BOTTOMS (WPC-1132)

USCGC JOSEPH DOYLE (WPC-1133)

USCGC WILLIAM HART (WPC-1134)

PATROL BOATS AND TRAINING CUTTERS

154' Sentinel Class Fast Response Cutter (WPC)
USCGC ANGELA MCSHAN (WPC-1135)
USCGC DANIEL TARR (WPC-1136)
USCGC EDGAR CULBERTSON (WPC-1137)
USCGC HAROLD MILLER (WPC-1138)
USCGC MYRTLE HAZARD (WPC-1139)
USCGC OLIVER HENRY (WPC-1140)
USCGC CHARLES MOULTHROPE (WPC-1141)
USCGC ROBERT GOLDMAN (WPC-1142)
USCGC FREDERICK HATCH (WPC-1143)
USCGC GLENN HARRIS (WPC-1144)
USCGC EMLEN TUNNELL (WPC-1145)
USCGC JOHN SCHEUERMAN (WPC-1146)
USCGC CLARENCE SUTPHIN (WPC-1147)
USCGC PABLO VALENT (WPC-1148)
USCGC DOUGLAS DENMAN (WPC-1149)
USCGC WILLIAM CHADWICK (WPC-1150)
USCGC WARREN DEYAMPERT (WPC-1151)
USCGC MAURICE JESTER (WPC-1152)
USCGC JOHN PATTERSON (WPC-1153)
USCGC WILLIAM SPARLING (WPC-1154)
USCGC MELVIN BELL (WPC-1155)
USCGC DAVID DUREN (WPC-1156)

125' Active Class Patrol Boat (Wix)
USCGC CUYAHOGA (WIX-157)

123' Patrol Boat (WPB)
USCGC MANITOU (WPB-1302)
USCGC MATAGORDA (WPB-1303)
USCGC MONHEGAN (WPB-1305)
USCGC NUNIVAK (WPB-1306)
USCGC VASHON (WPB-1308)
USCGC ATTU (WPB-1317)
USCGC METOMPKIN (WPB-1325)
USCGC PADRE (WPB-1328)

110' Surface Effect Ship (WSES)
USCGC DORADO (WSES-1)
USCGC SEA HAWK (WSES-2)
USCGC SHEARWATER (WSES-3)
USCGC PETREL (WSES-4)

110' Island Class Patrol Boat (WPB)
USCGC FARALLON (WPB-1301)
USCGC MAUI (WPB-1304)
USCGC OCRACOKE (WPB-1307)
USCGC AQUIDNECK (WPB-1309)
USCGC MUSTANG (WPB-1310)
USCGC NAUSHON (WPB-1311)

110' Island Class Patrol Boat (WPB)
USCGC SANIBEL (WPB-1312)
USCGC EDISTO (WPB-1313)
USCGC SAPELO (WPB-1314)
USCGC MATINICUS (WPB-1315)
USCGC NANTUCKET (WPB-1316)
USCGC BARANOF (WPB-1318)
USCGC CHANDELEUR (WPB-1319)
USCGC CHINCOTEAGUE (WPB-1320)
USCGC CUSHING (WPB-1321)
USCGC CUTTYHUNK (WPB-1322)
USCGC DRUMMOND (WPB-1323)
USCGC KEY LARGO (WPB-1324)
USCGC METOMPKIN (WPB-1325)
USCGC MONOMOY (WPB-1326)
USCGC ORCAS (WPB-1327)
USCGC SITKINAK (WPB-1329)
USCGC TYBEE (WPB-1330)
USCGC WASHINGTON (WPB-1331)
USCGC WRANGELL (WPB-1332)
USCGC ADAK (WPB-1333)
USCGC LIBERTY (WPB-1334)
USCGC ANACAPA (WPB-1335)

PATROL BOATS AND TRAINING CUTTERS

110' Island Class Patrol Boat (WPB)

USCGC KISKA (WPB-1336)

USCGC ASSATEAGUE (WPB-1337)

USCGC GRAND ISLE (WPB-1338)

USCGC KEY BISCAYNE (WPB-1339)

USCGC JEFFERSON ISLAND (WPB-1340)

USCGC KODIAK ISLAND (WPB-1341)

USCGC LONG ISLAND (WPB-1342)

USCGC BAINBRIDGE ISLAND (WPB-1343)

USCGC BLOCK ISLAND (WPB-1344)

USCGC STATEN ISLAND (WPB-1345)

USCGC ROANOKE ISLAND (WPB-1346)

USCGC PEA ISLAND (WPB-1347)

USCGC KNIGHT ISLAND (WPB-1348)

USCGC GALVESTON ISLAND (WPB-1349)

95' Cape Class Cutter (WPB)

USCGC CAPE SMALL (WPB-95300)

USCGC CAPE CORAL (WPB-95301)

USCGC CAPE HIGGON (WPB-95302)

USCGC CAPE UPRIGHT (WPB-95303)

USCGC CAPE GULL (WPB-95304)

USCGC CAPE HATTERAS (WPB-95305)

USCGC CAPE GEORGE (WPB-95306)

USCGC CAPE CURRENT (WPB-95307)

USCGC CAPE STRAIT (WPB-95308)

USCGC CAPE CARTER (WPB-95309)

USCGC CAPE WASH (WPB-95310)

USCGC CAPE HEDGE (WPB-95311)

USCGC CAPE KNOX (WPB-95312)

USCGC CAPE MORGAN (WPB-95313)

USCGC CAPE FAIRWEATHER (WPB-95314)

USCGC LA CRETE A PIERROT (WPB-95315)

USCGC CAPE FOX (WPB-95316)

USCGC CAPE JELLISON (WPB-95317)

USCGC CAPE NEWAGEN (WPB-95318)

USCGC CAPE ROMAIN (WPB-95319)

USCGC CAPE STARR (WPB-95320)

USCGC CAPE CROSS (WPB-95321)

USCGC CAPE HORN (WPB-95322)

USCGC CAPE DARBY (WPB-95323)

USCGC CAPE SHOALWATER (WPB-95324)

USCGC CAPE FLORIDA (WPB-95325)

USCGC CAPE CORWIN (WPB-95326)

USCGC CAPE PORPOISE (WPB-95327)

USCGC CAPE HENLOPEN (WPB-95328)

USCGC CAPE KIWANDA (WPB-95329)

USCGC CAPE FALCON (WPB-95330)

USCGC CAPE TRINITY (WPB-95331)

USCGC CAPE YORK (WPB-95332)

USCGC CAPE ROSIER (WPB-95333)

USCGC CAPE SABLE (WPB-95334)

USCGC CAPE PROVIDENCE (WPB-95335)

87' Marine Protector Class Patrol Boat (WPB)

USCGC BLACKFIN (WPB-87317)

USCGC BLUEFIN (WPB-87318)

USCGC YELLOWFIN (WPB-87319)

USCGC MANTA (WPB-87320)

USCGC COHO (WPB-87321)

USCGC KINGFISHER (WPB-87322)

USCGC SEAHAWK (WPB-87323)

USCGC STEELHEAD (WPB-87324)

USCGC BELUGA (WPB-87325)

USCGC BLACKTIP (WPB-87326)

USCGC PELICAN (WPB-87327)

USCGC RIDLEY (WPB-87328)

USCGC COCHITO (WPB-87329)

USCGC MANOWAR (WPB-87330)

USCGC MORAY (WPB-87331)

PATROL BOATS AND TRAINING CUTTERS

87' Marine Protector Class Patrol Boat (WPB)
USCGC RAZORBILL (WPB-87332)
USCGC ADELIE (WPB-87333)
USCGC GANNET (WPB-87334)
USCGC NARWHAL (WPB-87335)
USCGC STURGEON (WPB-87336)
USCGC SOCKEYE (WPB-87337)
USCGC IBIS (WPB-87338)
USCGC POMPANO (WPB-87339)
USCGC HALIBUT (WPB-87340)
USCGC BONITO (WPB-87341)
USCGC SHRIKE (WPB-87342)
USCGC TERN (WPB-87343)
USCGC HERON (WPB-87344)
USCGC WAHOO (WPB-87345)
USCGC FLYINGFISH (WPB-87346)
USCGC HADDOCK (WPB-87347)
USCGC BRANT (WPB-87348)
USCGC SHEARWATER (WPB-87349)
USCGC PETREL (WPB-87350)
USCGC SEA LION (WPB-87352)

USCGC SKIPJACK (WPB-87353)
USCGC DOLPHIN (WPB-87354)
USCGC HAWK (WPB-87355)
USCGC SAILFISH (WPB-87356)
USCGC SAWFISH (WPB-87357)
USCGC SWORDFISH (WPB-87358)
USCGC TIGER SHARK (WPB-87359)
USCGC BLUE SHARK (WPB-87360)
USCGC SEA HORSE (WPB-87361)
USCGC SEA OTTER (WPB-87362)
USCGC MANATEE (WPB-87363)
USCGC AHI (WPB-87364)
USCGC PIKE (WPB-87365)
USCGC TERRAPIN (WPB-87366)
USCGC SEA DRAGON (WPB-87367)
USCGC SEA DEVIL (WPB-87368)
USCGC CROCODILE (WPB-87369)
USCGC DIAMONDBACK (WPB-87370)
USCGC REEF SHARK (WPB-87371)
USCGC ALLIGATOR (WPB-87372)

82' Point Class Patrol Boat (WPB)
USCGC POINT ARDEN (WPB-82309)
USCGC POINT ARENA (WPB-82346)
USCGC POINT BAKER (WPB-82342)
USCGC POINT BANKS (WPB-82327)
USCGC POINT BARNES (WPB-82371)
USCGC POINT BARROW (WPB-82348)
USCGC POINT BATAN (WPB-82340)
USCGC POINT BENNETT (WPB-82351)
USCGC POINT BONITA (WPB-82347)
USCGC POINT BRIDGE (WPB-82338)
USCGC POINT BROWER (WPB-82372)
USCGC POINT BROWN (WPB-82362)
USCGC POINT CAMDEN (WPB-82373)
USCGC POINT CARREW (WPB-82374)
USCGC POINT CAUTION (WPB-82301)
USCGC POINT CHARLES (WPB-82361)
USCGC POINT CHICO (WPB-82339)
USCGC POINT CLEAR (WPB-82315)
USCGC POINT COMFORT (WPB-82317)
USCGC POINT COUNTESS (WPB-82335)
USCGC POINT CYPRESS (WPB-82326)

PATROL BOATS AND TRAINING CUTTERS

82' Point Class Patrol Boat (WPB)

USCGC POINT DIVIDE (WPB-82337)
USCGC POINT DORAN (WPB-82375)
USCGC POINT DUME (WPB-82325)
USCGC POINT ELLIS (WPB-82330)
USCGC POINT ESTERO (WPB-82344)
USCGC POINT EVANS (WPB-82354)
USCGC POINT FRANCIS (WPB-82356)
USCGC POINT FRANKLIN (WPB-82350)
USCGC POINT GAMMON (WPB-82328)
USCGC POINT GARNET (WPB-82310)
USCGC POINT GLASS (WPB-82336)
USCGC POINT GLOVER (WPB-82307)
USCGC POINT GRACE (WPB-82323)
USCGC POINT GREY (WPB-82324)
USCGC POINT HANNON (WPB-82355)
USCGC POINT HARRIS (WPB-82376)
USCGC POINT HERRON (WPB-82318)
USCGC POINT HEYER (WPB-82369)
USCGC POINT HIGHLAND (WPB-82333)
USCGC POINT HOBART (WPB-82377)
USCGC POINT HOPE (WPB-82302)
USCGC POINT HUDSON (WPB-82322)
USCGC POINT HURON (WPB-82357)

USCGC POINT JACKSON (WPB-82378)
USCGC POINT JEFFERSON (WPB-82306)
USCGC POINT JUDITH (WPB-82345)
USCGC POINT KENNEDY (WPB-82320)
USCGC POINT KNOLL (WPB-82367)
USCGC POINT LEAGUE (WPB-82304)
USCGC POINT LEDGE (WPB-82334)
USCGC POINT LOBOS (WPB-82366)
USCGC POINT LOMAS (WPB-82321)
USCGC POINT LOOKOUT (WPB-82341)
USCGC POINT MARONE (WPB-82331)
USCGC POINT MARTIN (WPB-82379)
USCGC POINT MAST (WPB-82316)
USCGC POINT MONROE (WPB-82353)
USCGC POINT NOWELL (WPB-82363)
USCGC POINT ORIENT (WPB-82319)
USCGC POINT PARTRIDGE (WPB-82305)
USCGC POINT RICHMOND (WPB-82370)
USCGC POINT ROBERTS (WPB-82332)
USCGC POINT SAL (WPB-82352)
USCGC POINT SLOCUM (WPB-82313)
USCGC POINT SPENCER (WPB-82349)

USCGC POINT STEELE (WPB-82359) (EX-POINT BUCHON)
USCGC POINT STUART (WPB-82358)
USCGC POINT SWIFT (WPB-82312)
USCGC POINT THATCHER (WPB-82314)
USCGC POINT TURNER (WPB-82365) (EX-POINT HOUGHTON)
USCGC POINT VERDE (WPB-82311)
USCGC POINT WARDE (WPB-82368)
USCGC POINT WELCOME (WPB-82329)
USCGC POINT WELLS (WPB-82343)
USCGC POINT WHITE (WPB-82308)
USCGC POINT WHITEHORN (WPB-82364)
USCGC POINT WINSLOW (WPB-82360)
USCGC POINT YOUNG (WPB-82303)

USCG Signalman First Class Douglas Munro volunteered to support the Navy during the 1942 landings at Guadalcanal. When one group of Marines came under a massive Japanese counterattack while assaulting a beachhead, Munro led the evacuation of the Marine force.

While the Marines were loading onto the evacuation boats, Munro placed his boat between them and the incoming fire to protect the Marines. Munro then moved his boat to free one that had run aground before he was shot in the head by a Japanese machine gun.

Munro posthumously received the Medal of Honor for his actions in rescuing the Marines on Guadalcanal, and his medal currently has a place of honor in the National Museum of the Marine Corps.

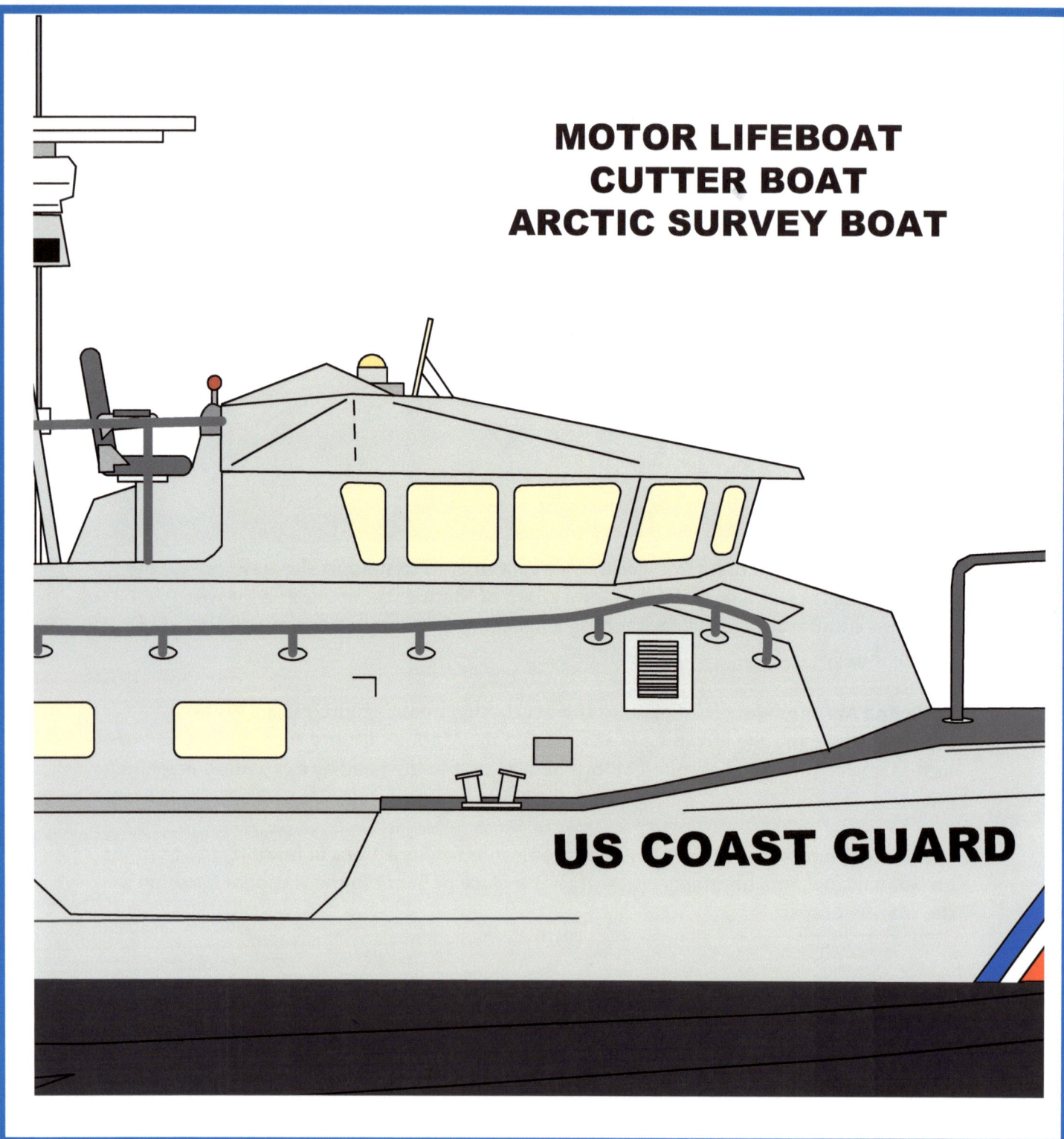

MLB	Motor LifeBoat
SRB	Surf Rescue Boat
MSB	Motor Surfboat

The National Motor Lifeboat School is a "C" class school located near the mouth of the Columbia River at Cape Disappointment just outside of Ilwaco, WA. It's also known as the "Graveyard of the Pacific. Coxswains completing the course will be authorized to wear a Heavy Weather Coxswain or MLB Surfman pin.

ASB	Arctic Survey Boat
BB-L	Cutter Boat Large
CB-M	Cutter Boat Medium
CB-S	Cutter Boat Smal
CB-OTH	Over the Horizon boat
TCB	Motor Cargo Boat

The 26 ft motor surf boat was the mainstay on the cutters since the 70's, 80's, and 90's. There was a shift to more capable boats that can operate farther away from the cutter. The over the horizon boats (CB-OTH) have electronics and communications that allow them to extend the distance from the cutter. The addition of stern ramps has allowed larger cutter boats the be carried and the ability to launch while underway at 4-5 knots.

25 FOOT MOTOR SURFBOAT (MSB SV)

Number   253301 through 253317
Completed   1969-1970
Cost $16,300 (1967)

Over the period of 1969 to 1970, a total of 17 boats were built or modified mark 1 types to the shore version (CG-253301-253317). Most of these were assigned to Atlantic and Pacific coast stations located at inlet entrances.

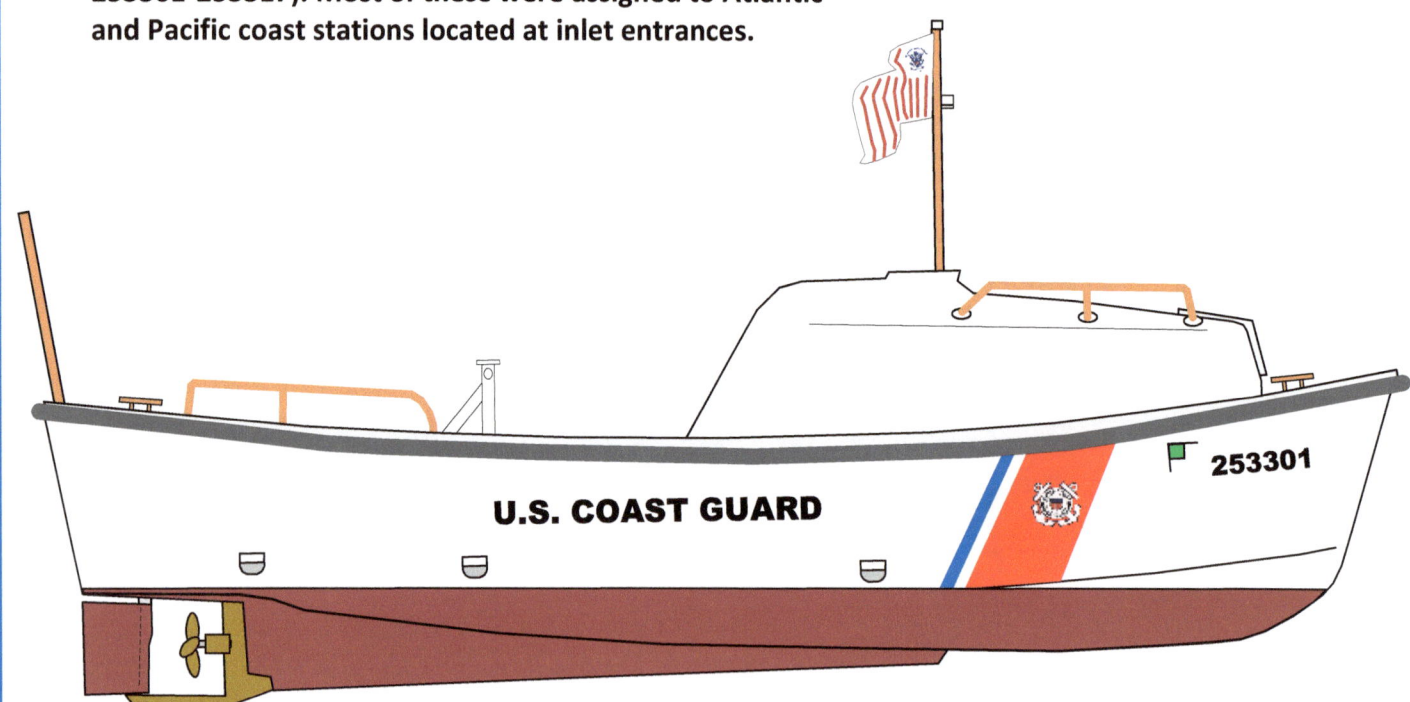

Displacement	7,410 fully loaded (lbs)
Length	25' 8" Beam: 7' 1" Draft: 2' 1"
Main Engines:	1 General Motors diesel BHP: 80
Performance	Max Sustained: 11 knots, 60 mile radius
Fuel Oil	30 (95%)
Complement	3

30 FOOT SURF RESCUE CRAFT (SRB)

Number	30201 through 30220
Built	Willard Boat Company Fountain Valley, CA 1986-1990
Number built	20

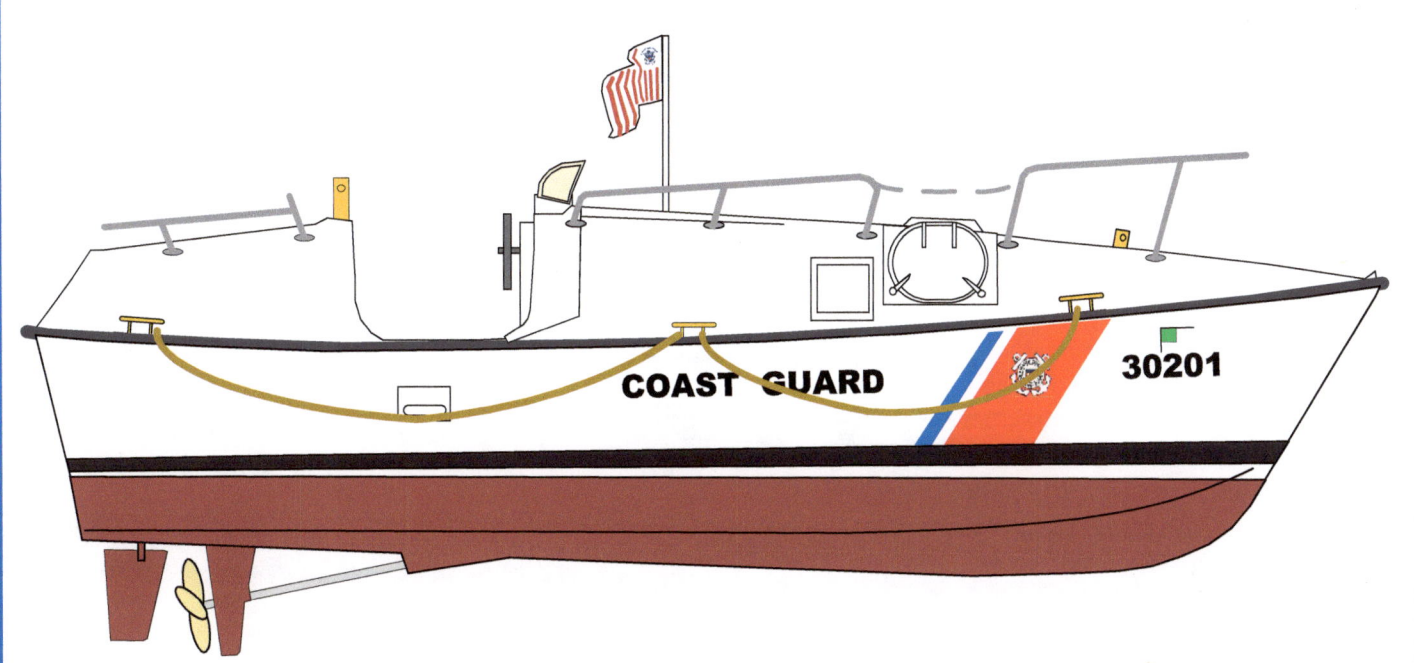

Displacement	11,500 (lbs) fully loaded
Length	30' 4" (max) Beam 9' 4" (max) Draft: 3' 8" (max)
single	6V92TI engine 375 horsepower
Fuel Oil	77 gallons (95%)
Performance	Max Speed: 31 knots
	Cruising: 25 knots
	155 mile radius
Complement	2 men

36 FOOT MOTOR LIFEBOAT TYPE T, TR AND TRS (MLB)

Builder	Coast Guard Yard in Curtis Bay, Md
built	between 1929 and 1956
	218 type T, TR and TRS
Cost:	$18,912 per boat (1945)
	$15,250 (1930)

Serving the Coast Guard and the Life Saving Services for almost 100 years, the last one, CG-36535, serving Depoe Bay MLB Station in Oregon until 1987.

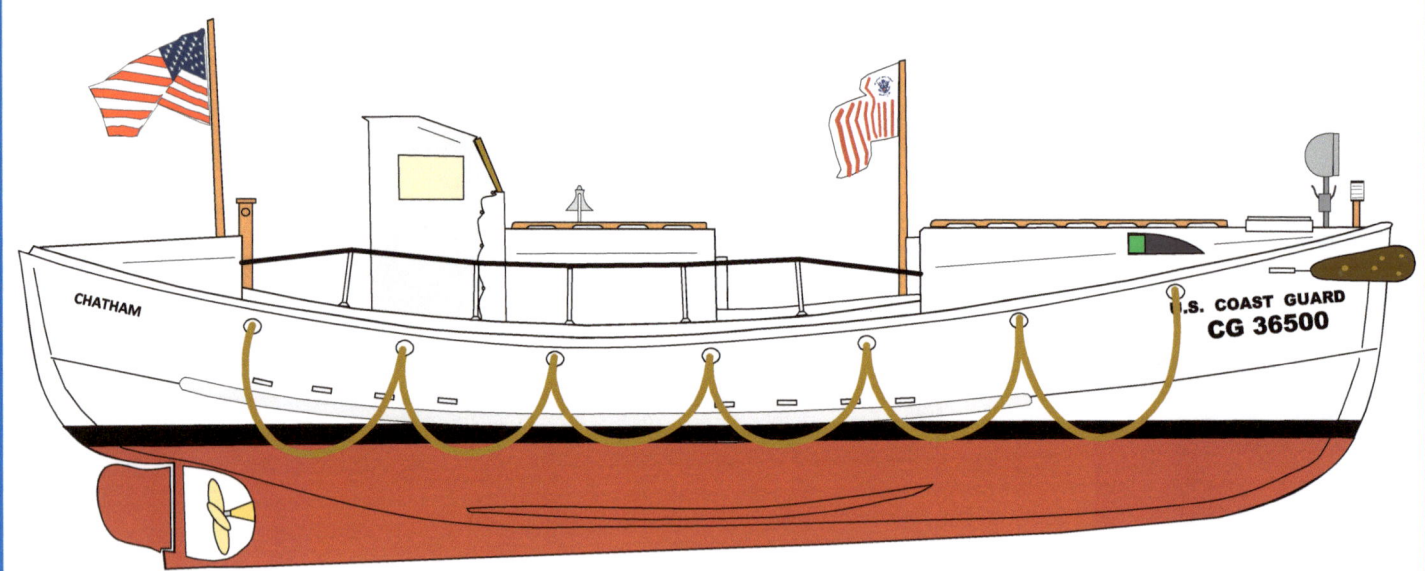

Displacement	20,170 lbs.
Length	36'8" Beam 10'9" max Draft 3'4"
Powerplant	1x Sterling "Petrel" 90 hp @ 1,000 rpm gasoline engine.
	1x 75 – 100 hp diesel engine Single screw.
Dax Speed	9 knots (sustained)
Endurance	280 mi @ 8 kts. 202 mi @ 9 kts.
Complement	Crew: 3 Passengers: 20 – 30

42 FOOT SPECIAL PURPOSE CRAFT-NEARSHORE LIFEBOAT (SPC-NLB)

Built by Safe Boats Between 2008 and 2011 Numbered 42001-42003

There are only three 42 SPC-NLBs, and they were procured specifically for the challenging conditions at Station Chatham, Massachusetts, where the shallow water harbor entrances prevent the 47 MLBs from operating.

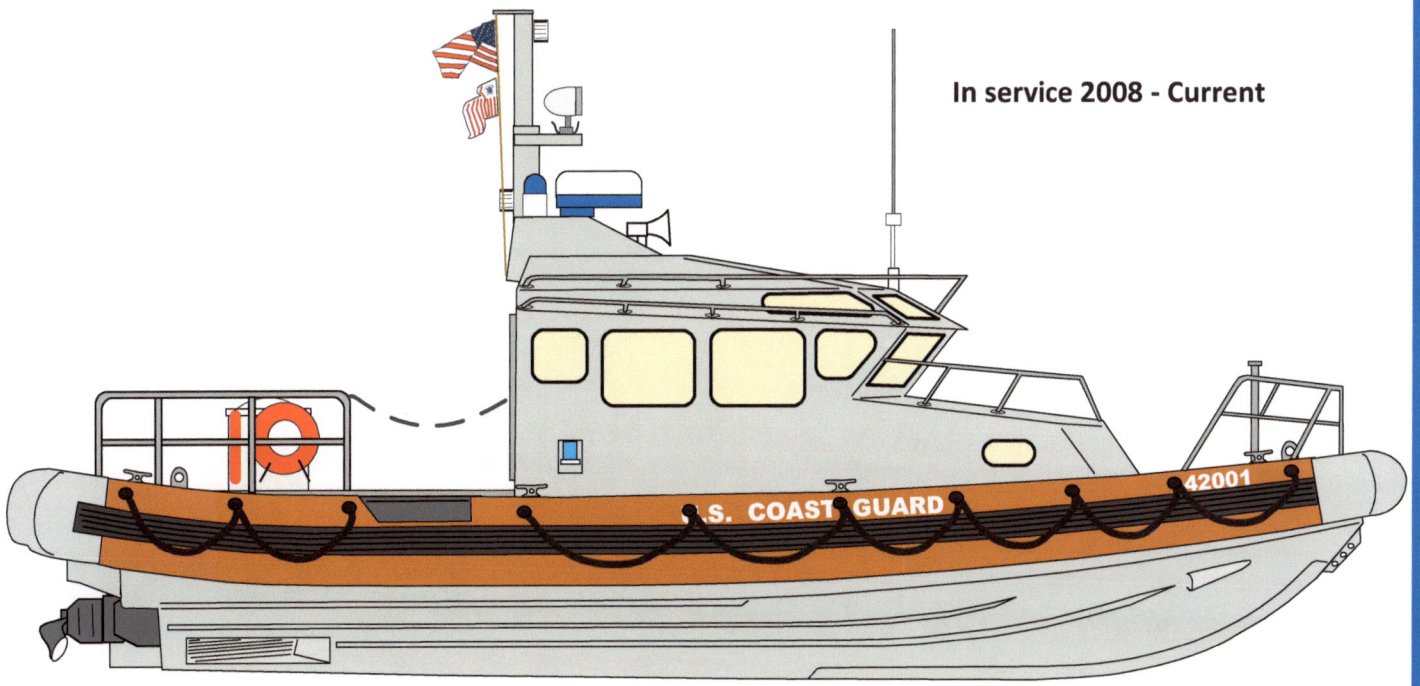

In service 2008 - Current

Length	42.8 Beam 13.8 8.4
Speed	30 knots max Cruising 25 knots
Range	250 mn at 35 kts
Maximum Winds	50 knots
Maximum Seas	20 ft
Maximum Surf	15 ft
Towing Capacity	100 tons

44 FOOT MOTOR LIFEBOAT (MLB)

Builder	Coast Guard yard Curtis bay MD
Number	44300 through 44409
Completed	7 January 1963 to November 1972
Built	110
Cost	$125,000 (1967)
	$225,000 (1972)

In service 1963 - 2010

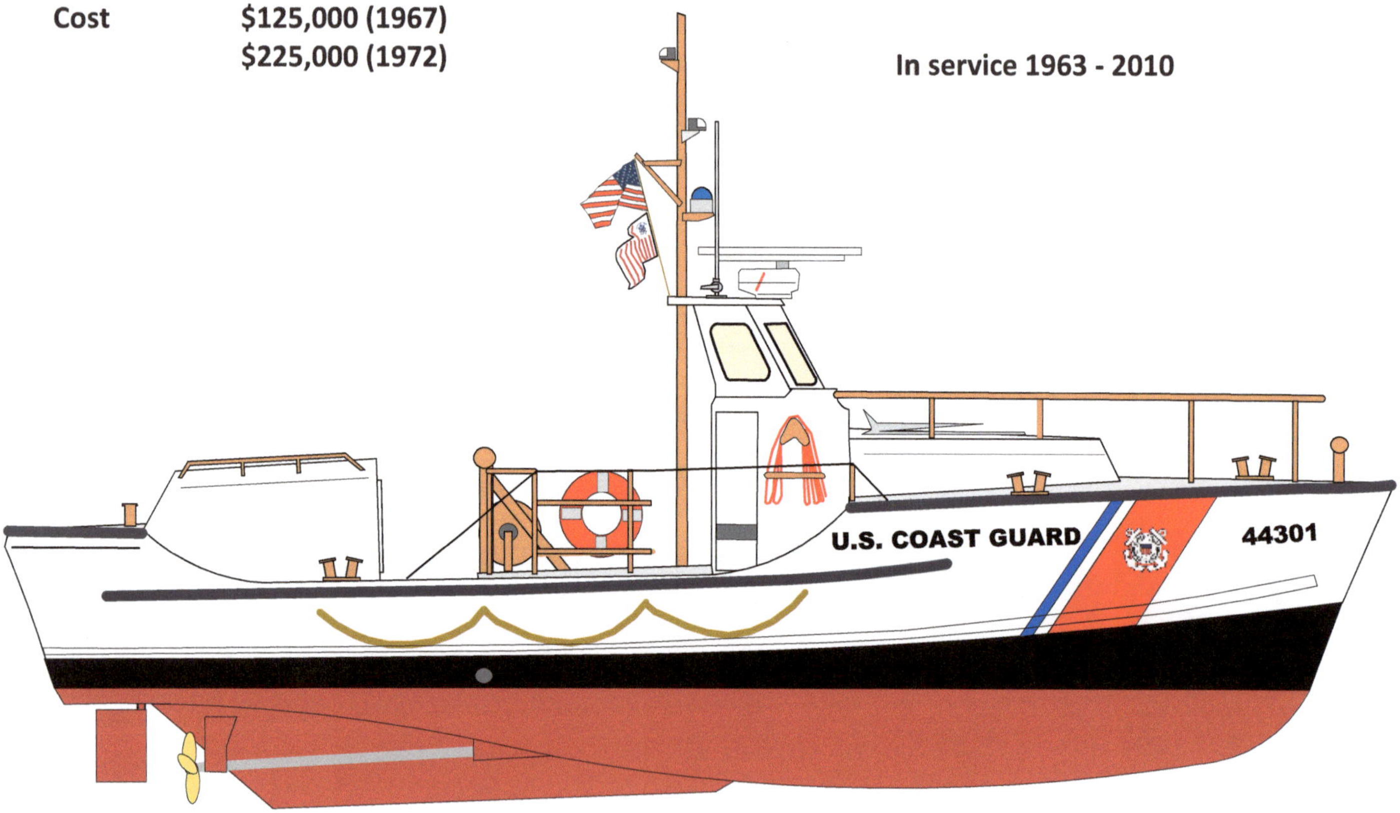

Displacement	20 tons (fully loaded) (1972)
Length	44' 2" Beam 12' 8"
Main Engines	2 Detroit diesels BHP: 370
Propellers	twin
Max Sustained	14 knots
Range	164 nm
Fuel Oil	330 gallons (95%)
Complement	4

47 FOOT MOTOR LIFEBOAT (MLB)

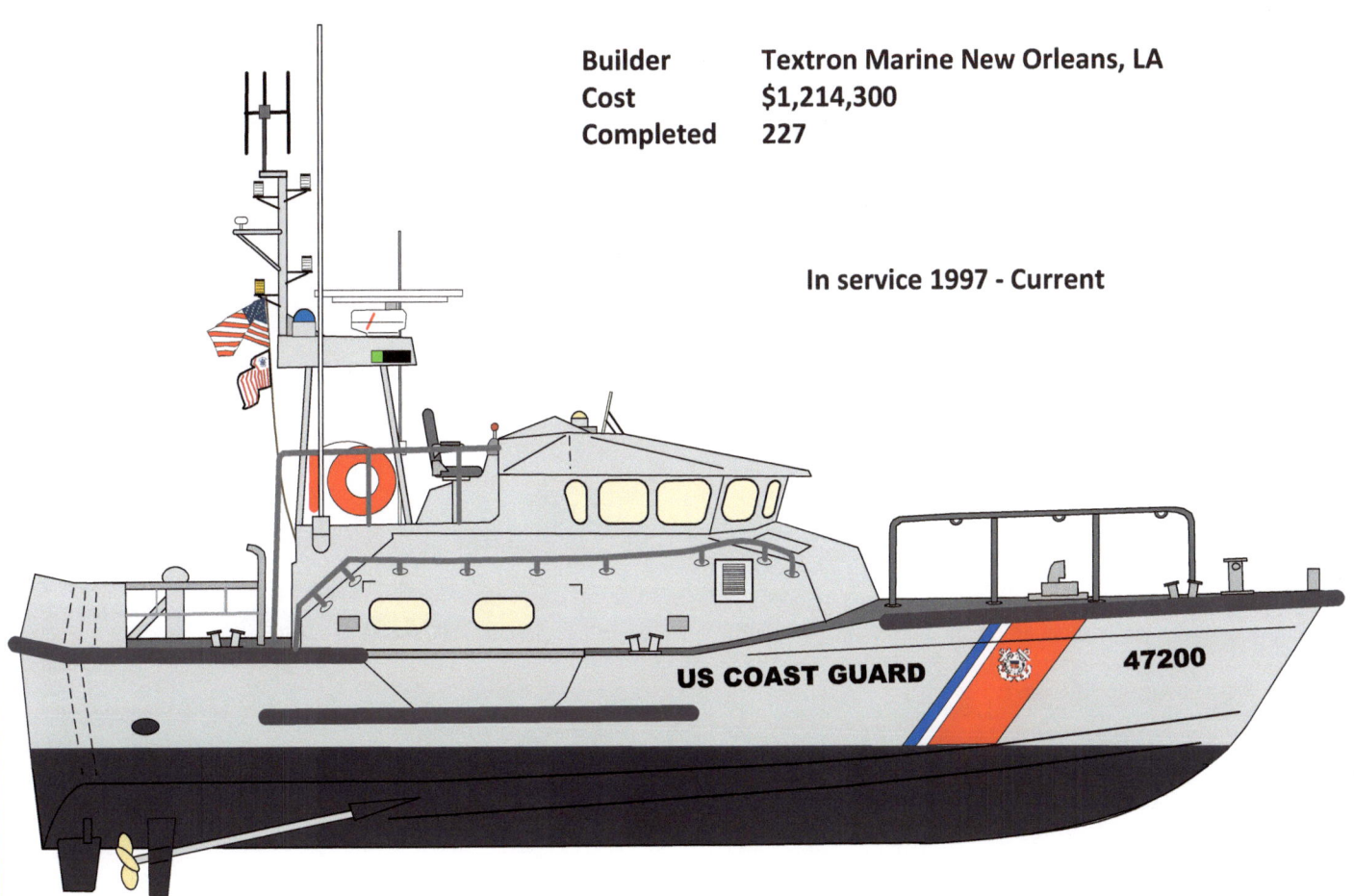

Builder	Textron Marine New Orleans, LA
Cost	$1,214,300
Completed	227

In service 1997 - Current

Displacement	18 ton
Length	47 ft 11 in Beam 14 ft Draft 14 ft 6 in
Power	2 × Detroit Diesel 6V92TA DDEC-IV engines, 435 hp each
Fuel capacity	373 usable gallons
Speed	25 knots maximum 22 knots cruising
Range	200 nm at cruise
Complement	4 crew 30 passengers
Armament	1 × M240B machine gun

52 FOOT MOTOR LIFEBOAT (MLB)

Builder Coast Guard yard Curtis Bay Baltimore, Md
Cost $236,000 (1962)

The 52' MLBs are the only vessels of the Coast Guard less than 65 feet in length to receive names

Victory	52312
Invincible II	52313
Triumph II	52314
Intrepid	52315

In service 1956 - 2021

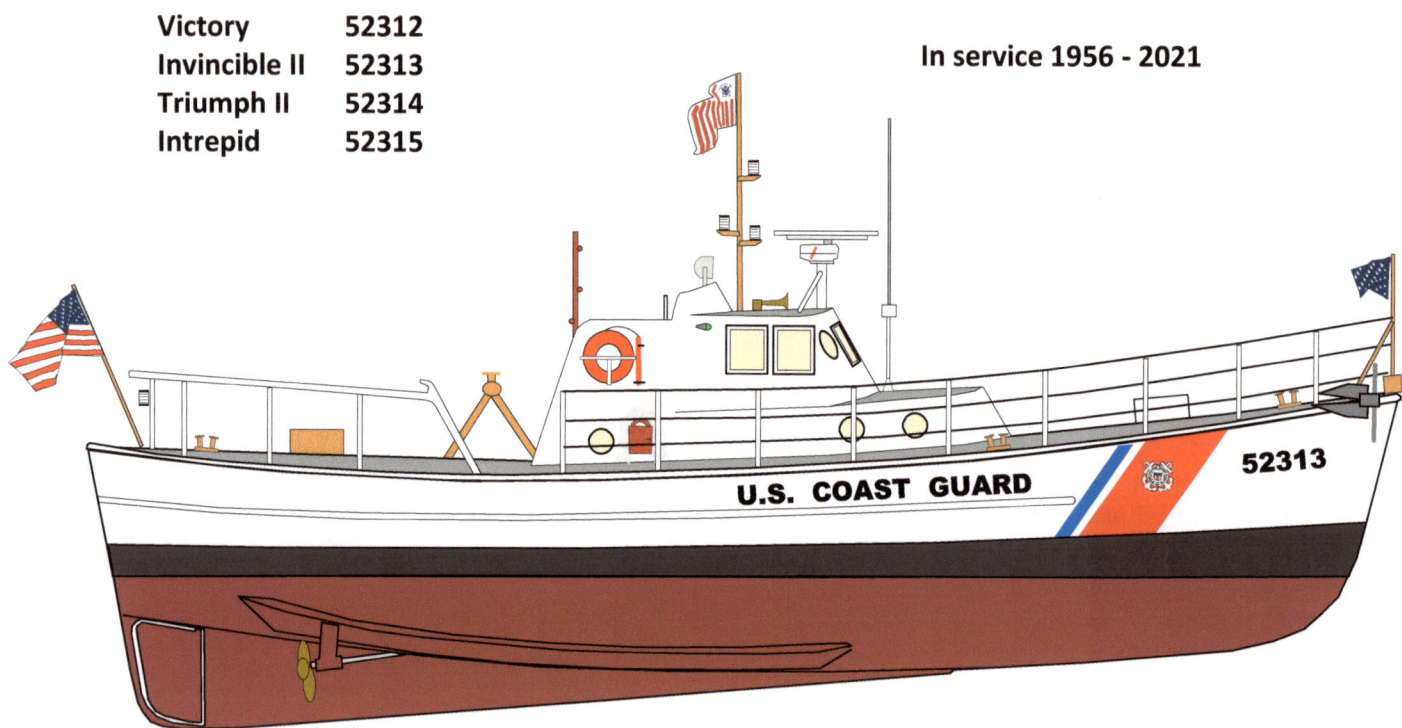

Displacement	32 tons
Length	52 feet Beam 14 feet 7 in Draught 6 feet 11 in
Propulsion	2×GM 6-71, 170 hp
Speed	11 knots
Range	495 nautical miles
Capacity	35 survivors + crew
Complement	5

self-righting and self-bailing capabilities and the ability to tow vessels as large as 750 long tons in 30-foot seas

all stationed in the Pacific Northwest

18 FOOT CUTTERBOAT AIDS TO NAVIGATION MEDIUM (CB-ATON-M)

Builder Metal Shark, Jeanerette, Louisiana

The United States Coast Guard awarded a single five year Indefinite Delivery Indefinite Quantity Firm-Fixed Price contract for up to 18 Cutter Boats - Aids to Navigation - Medium (CB-ATON-M)

CB-ATON-M are carried on board 175-foot Keeper Class Coastal Buoy Tenders (WLM)

In service 2016 - Current

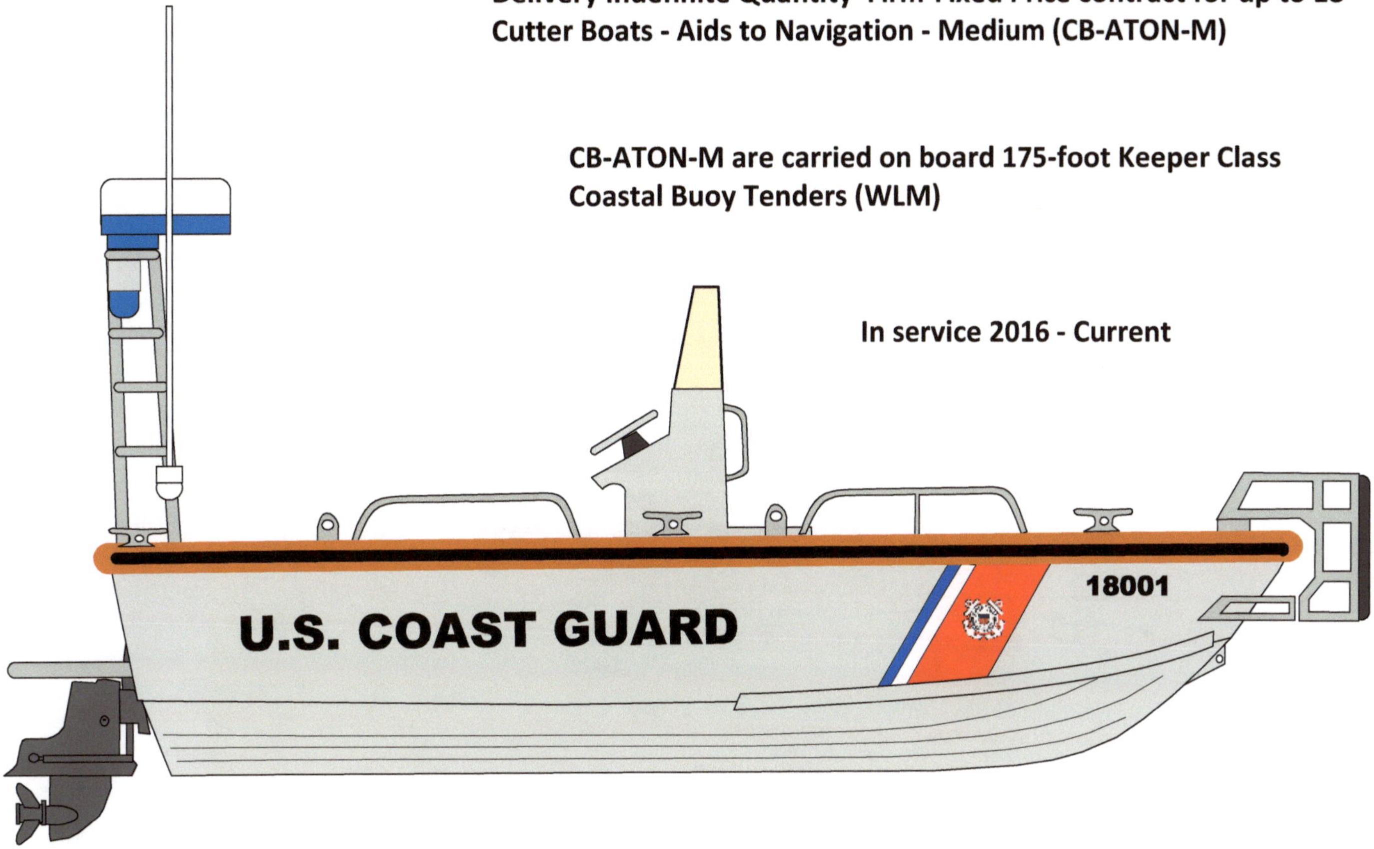

weight	2,500 lb
LOA	18 ft, beam 7 ft 6 in, draft 14 in
Power	Mercury Marine's 2.0 diesel engine Max hp 250
fuel	40 US gal

25 FOOT MOTOR CARGO BOAT (MCB)

Builder Coast Guard yard, Curtis Bay, MD
Cost 244,929 (1968)

Carried onboard cutters

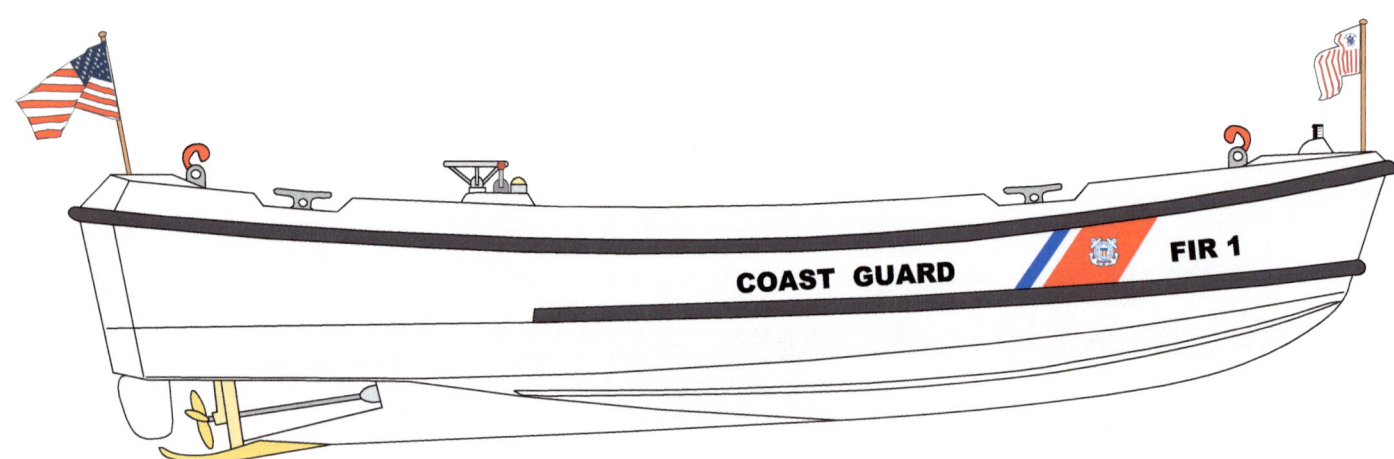

Displacement	8,594 lbs
Length	25'8" beam 7'11" draft 2'2"
Engine	3-53 Detroit diesel
Fuel capacity	40 gal
Speed	12 kts max, 12 kts cruise
Range	85 nm
Crew	3

26 FOOT CUTTER BOAT (OTHB)

VERSION IV

IV fourth generation is manufactured by SAFE Boats International of Port Orchard, Washington. It was part of a 101-boat order worth up to $58.9 million. It is an inboard/outboard design powered by a 500 hp Cummins diesel inboard engine with a Hamilton jet drive.

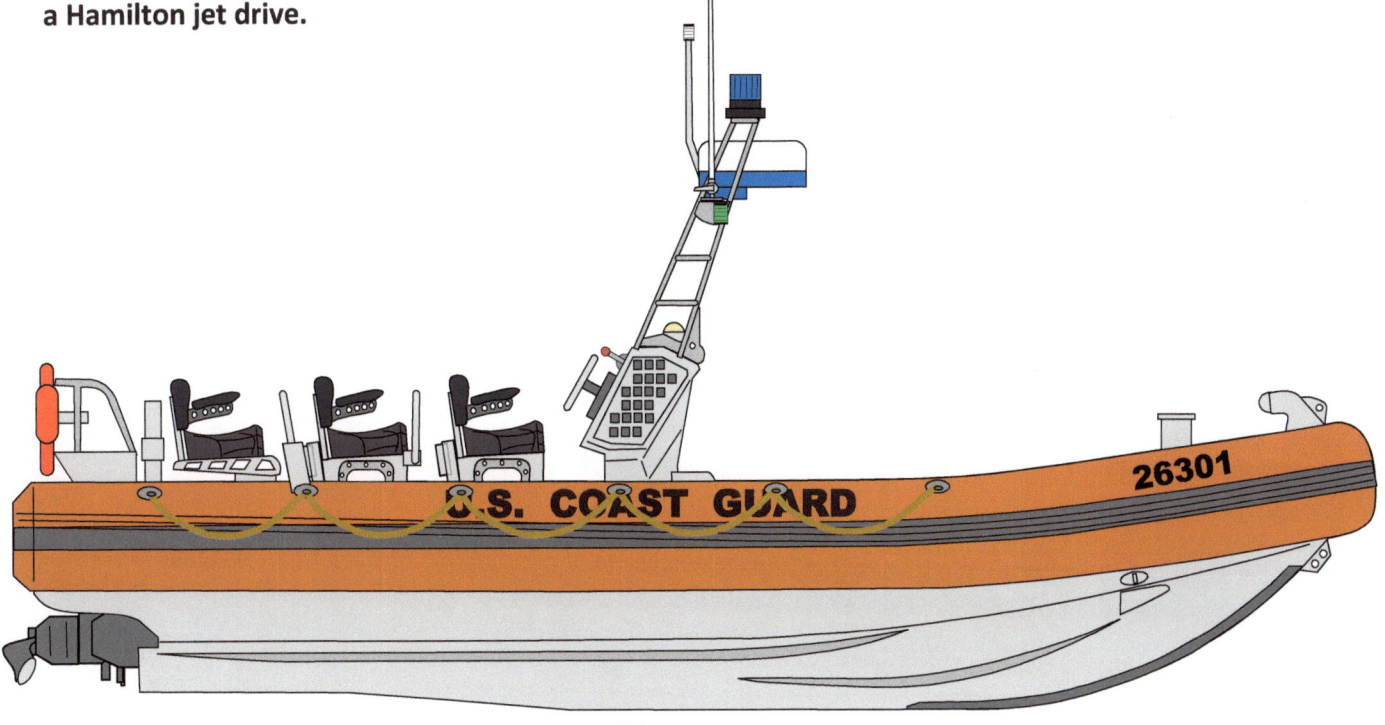

Length	26 feet
Power	single diesel engine water jet propelled
Speed	40 knots
Towing capacity	3,000 lbs pull on tow bit
Max winds	30 knots
Max wave height	11 feet

compatibility with both stern and side-davit launch and recovery systems.

26 FOOT CUTTER BOAT (CB-OTH)

VERSION V

A 10-year contract awarded to Inventech Marine Solutions of Bremerton, Washington, in August 2022. The contract supports delivery of up to 194 boats and has a total value of almost $100 million.

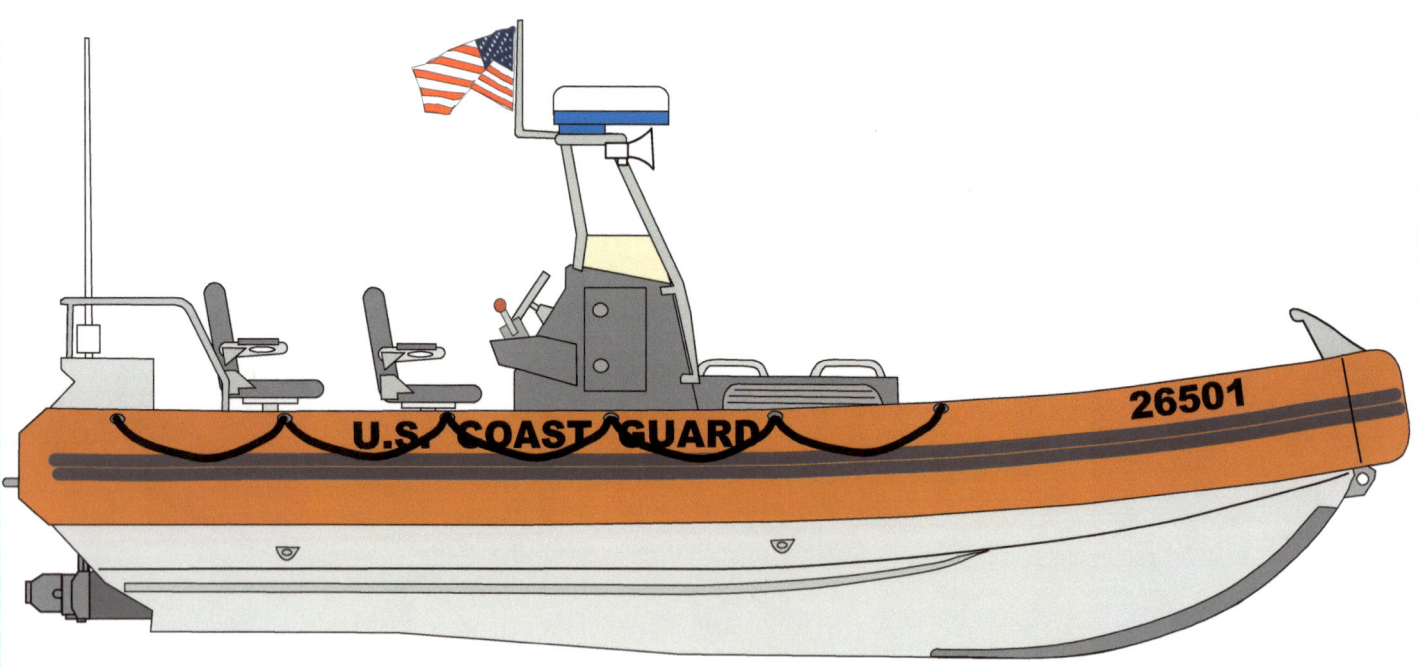

The OTH V is powered by a marine diesel engine and waterjet, with a top speed of approximately 40 knots and a range more than 170 nautical miles. The dimensions are limited to 26 feet long by 8.5 feet wide, with a maximum performance weight of 8,700 pounds, to ensure compatibility with the various Coast Guard cutters it will support.

26 FOOT MOTOR SURFBOAT (MSB)

Manufacturer	Ocean Technical Services, Harvey, LA
Completed	(shore-based + cutter-based) 300 1960-1990's

In service 1960 - 2000

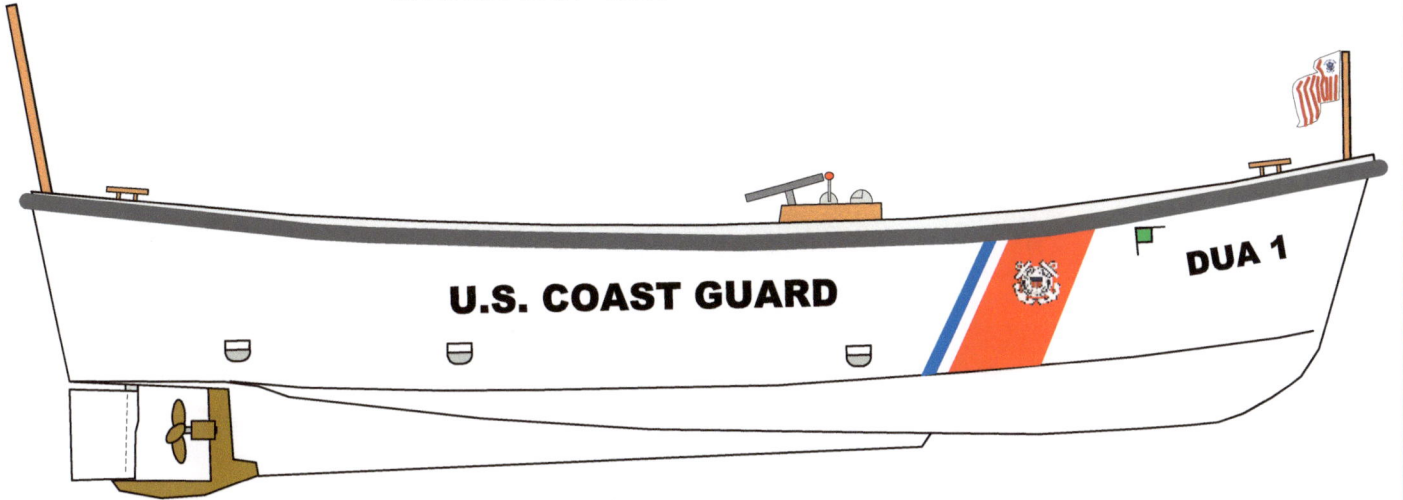

Displacement	5,000lbs
Length	25' 8"
Beam	13 ft. 6 in.
Draft	2 ft.
Propulsion	Single Screw Diesel, Cummins 4BT3.9M
Speed	18 knots max
Crew	3 plus 13 survivors

35 FOOT LONG RANGE INTERCEPTOR II CUTTER BOAT (LRI)

Built by MetalCraft Marine U.S. Inc Watertown, NY
12 total
Numbered 35101 - 35112

Stern launched aboard the National Security Cutter.

In service 2013 - Current

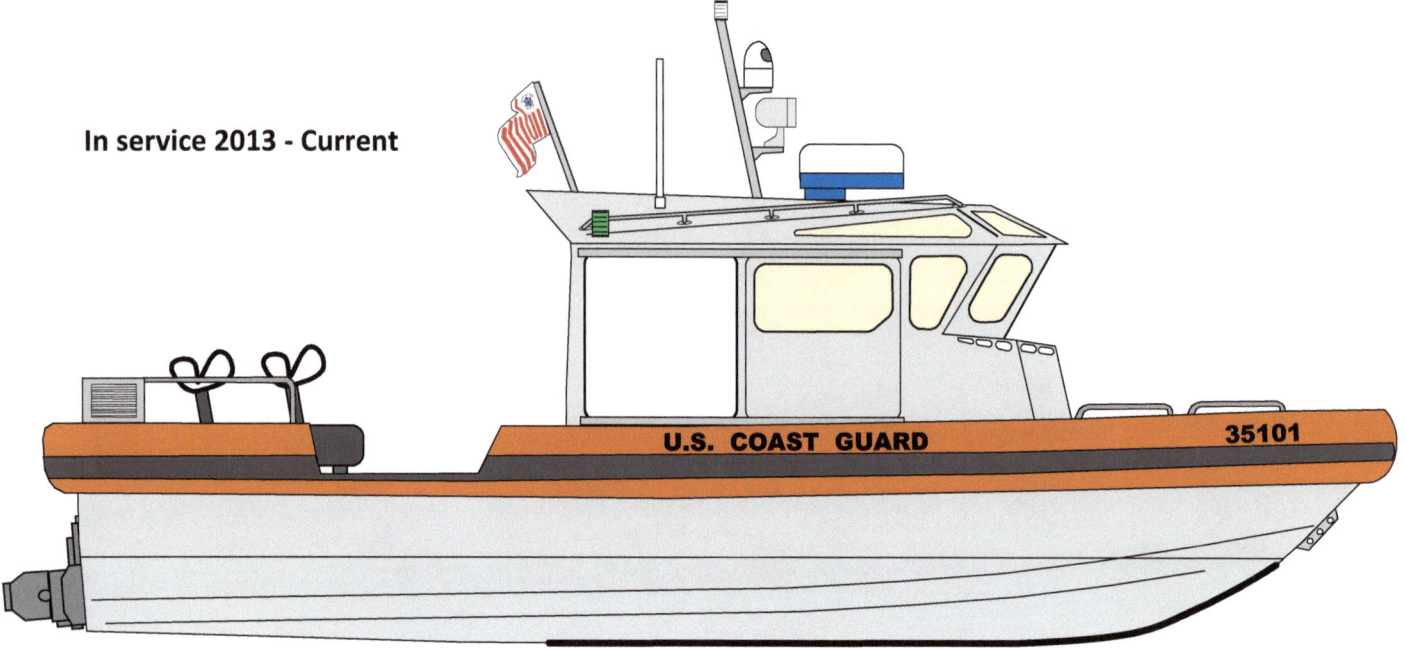

Length	35 feet Beam 11' 4"
Fuel	284 gallons
Power	two Cummins Tier III 6.7L diesel engines 480hp at 3,300rpm each. Engines burn JP-5 fuel or alternative bio-fuel and have a five-minute run dry capacity. Ultra 305 water jets with electronic joystick controls and ZF 280 PL transmission.
speed	42knots max
range	up to 236nmi
Maximum winds	21-25 knots
Towing capacity	10 gross tons

The boat can be launched and recovered up to sea state five.

38 FOOT ARCTIC SURVEY BOAT (ASB)

Builder Monson Burlington, WA

The 38-foot artic survey boat is aboard the Polar Class and Healy icebreakers and used to conduct science operations.

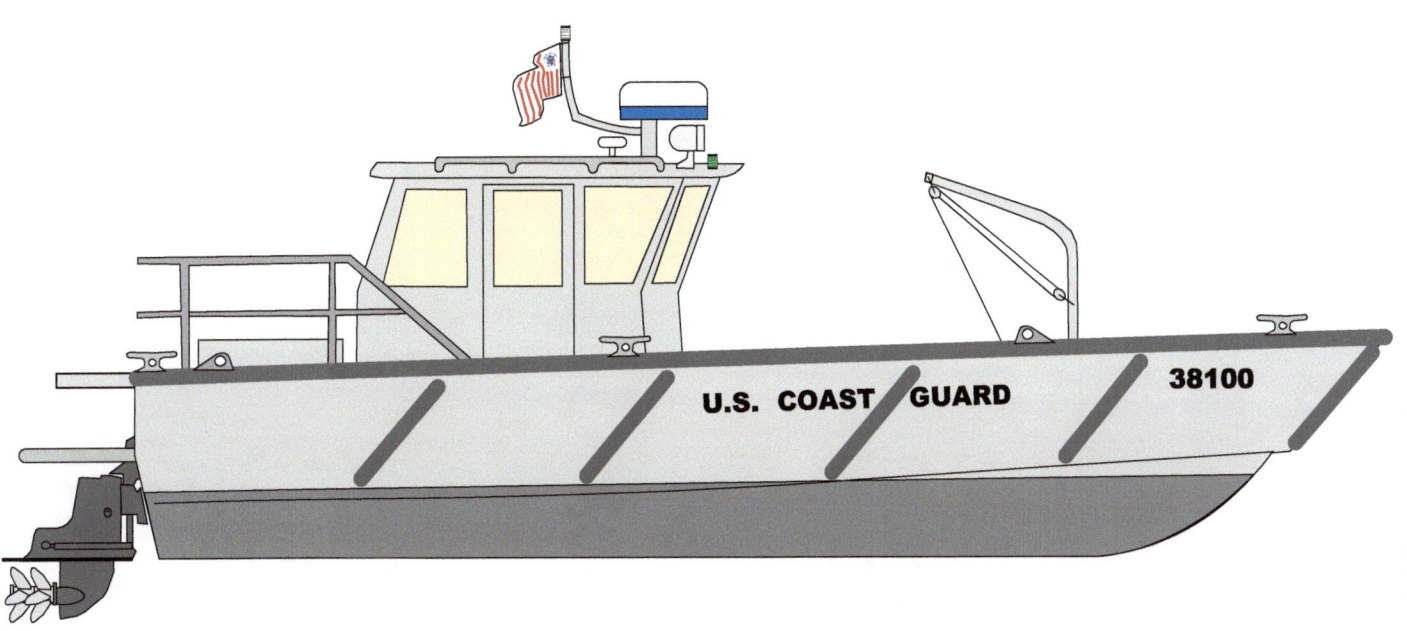

Length	38 feet 6 inches Beam 12 ft
Hull Type	Mono hull
Power	Volvo KAD43 230 hp x 2
Propulsion	Volvo Duoprop sterndrive
Speed	43 mph, light ship
Fuel	250 gallons

39 FOOT ARCTIC SURVEY BOAT (ASB)

Builder United Boat Building in Bellingham, WA
Built 1965
Reinforced fiberglass hull for minor ice-breaking

Constructed of a single skin fiberglass hull with a reinforced bow for minor icebreaking and a reinforced belt around the waterline for protection against ice fields.

Carried onboard wind, Glacier, and Polar class icebreakers.

Displacement 12 tons
length   39 ft beam of 11 ft 3 in draft 4 ft
Power   diesel inboard and diesel generator
Speed   12 knots
Complement up to 6

August 4th 1790. Congress authorized Secretary of the Treasury Alexander Hamilton's proposal to build ten cutters to protect the new nation's revenue. Alternately known as the system of cutters, Revenue Service, and Revenue-Marine this service would officially be named the Revenue Cutter Service in 1863. The cutters were placed under the control of the Treasury Department. This date marks the officially recognized birthday of the Coast Guard.

The service received its present name in 1915 under an act of Congress when the Revenue Cutter Service merged with the Life-Saving Service. The nation then had a single maritime service dedicated to saving life at sea and enforcing the nation's maritime laws.

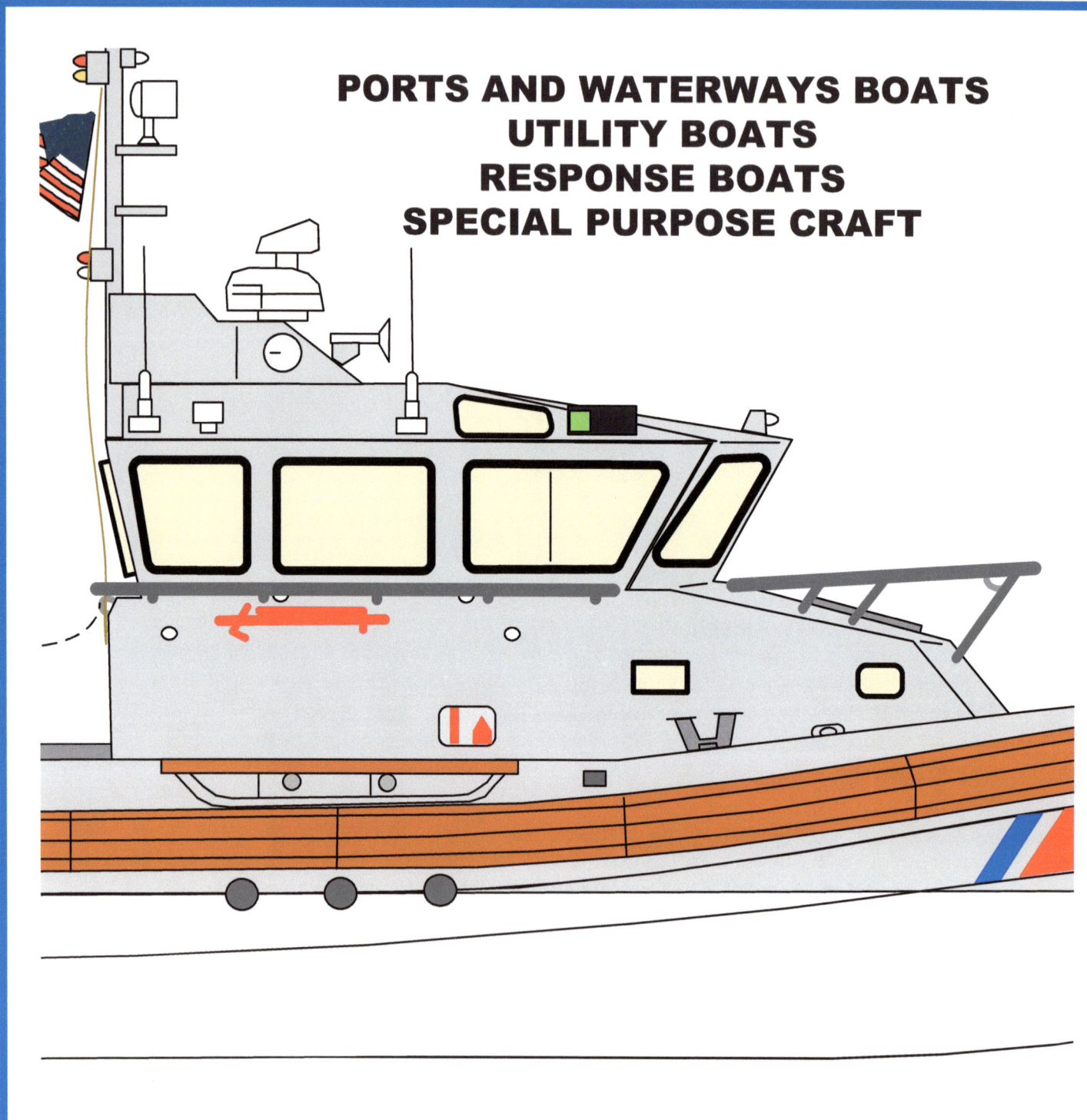

PWB	**Ports and Waterways Boat**
PWM	**Ports and Waterways, Medium**
TPSB	**Transportable Port Security Boat**

The Port and Waterways Act of 1973 assigned the Coast Guard the responsibility for safety in these waters. The act included major ports and harbors. The early boats were assigned to reserve units up and down the coast. The 31-foot PWB's ended up at Boatswains mate "A" school in Yorktown VA. teaching students single screw boat handling.

UTB	**Utility Boat**
UTL	**Utility Boat, Light**
RB-M	**Response Boat-Medium**
RB-S	**Response Boat-Small**
DPB	**Deployable Pursuit Boat**
SPC	**Special Purpose Craft**
LARC	**Amphibious rescue craft**
PSD	**Presidential security boat**
FCI	**Fast coastal interceptor**

The workhorse of the Coast Guard, the utility boats performed general use in search and rescue, as well as for law enforcement, nearshore patrol, and logistics duties. The 41 UTB Large was one of the most successful and most recognizable Coast Guard vessels replacing the 40 ft mark IV's. The Response boat – medium replaced the 41's and unlike the 41-foot utility boat, the RB-M can self-right if it should ever capsize. Special purpose craft are mission and location specific to the needs of the station. The FCI was a short-lived program designed to help stations in Southern Florida battle the drug war.

25 FOOT TRANSPORTABLE PORT SECURITY BOAT (TPSB)

Builder Boston Whaler Edgewater, Fl 1996-99
Numbered 25300-25343

Length	24 ft 7 in Beam 7 ft 10 in Draught 3 ft 3.0 in
Propulsion	2 × Evinrude outboard engines, 175 hp each
Speed	50 knots maximum
Armament	2 × M240B 7.62mm machine gun
	1 x M2HB .50-caliber machine gun
Complement	3

25 FOOT DEFENDER RB-HS (C CLASS)

A Class   Search and rescue, Security Response Team (MSRT)
B Class   Search and rescue, law enforcement
C Class   Port Security Units

Builders   A class   SAFE Boats International
            B and C Class   Metal Shark Boats

Completed   over 700 all classes

Displacement	8.5 long tons
Length	29 ft 6 in Beam 8 ft 6 in Draught 3 ft 3 in
Propulsion	2 × Honda 4-stroke outboard engines, 225 hp (168 kW) each
Speed	46 knots max 35 knots cruising
Range	150 nm
Complement	4 crew, 6 passengers
Armament	1 × M2HB, 2 × M240B M60 machine gun

31 FOOT PORT SECURITY BOAT (PSB)

Builder CG Yard Curtis Bay, MD CG-31005 - CG-31019
Numbered 31005 through 31028
Cost $55,051 (1969)

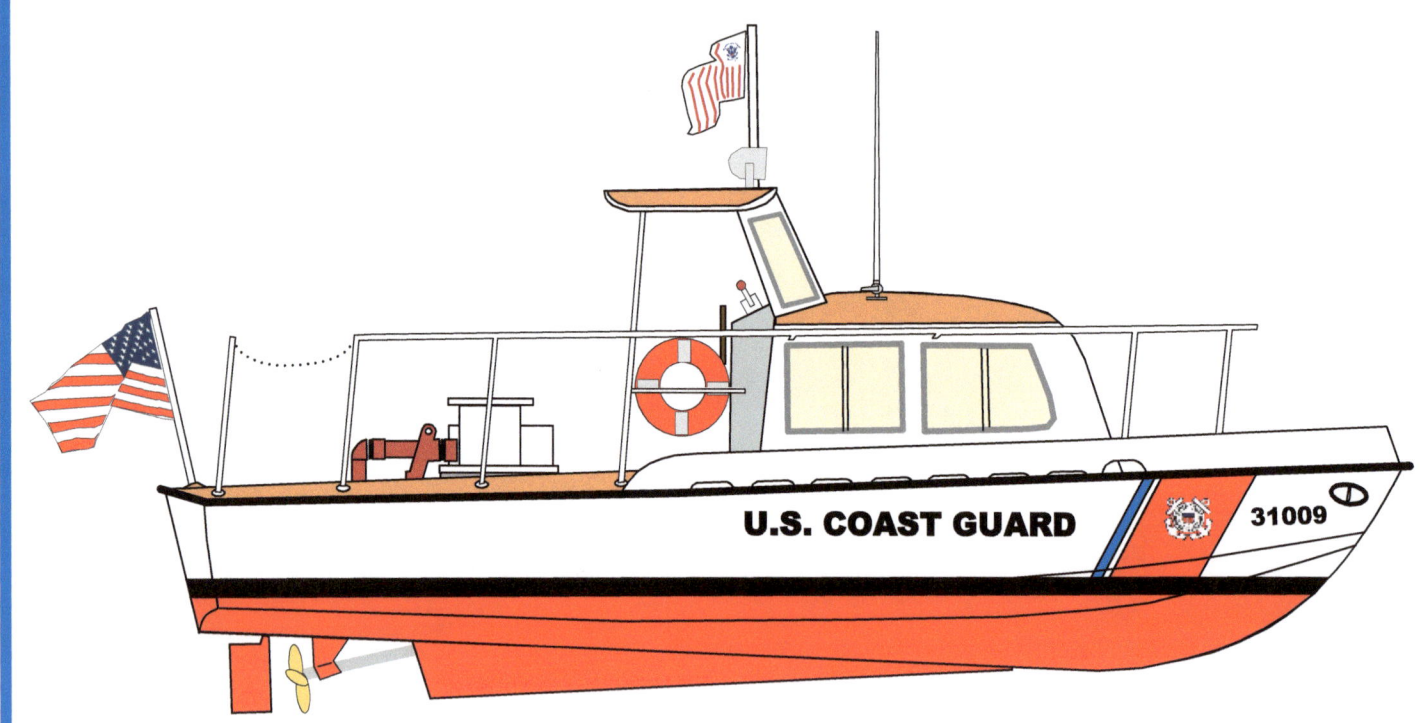

Displacement	16,285 (lbs)
Length	30' 5" Beam 11' 6" max
Draft	3' 11" max (1980)
Main Engines	1 General Motors diesel 197 HP
Max Speed	14 knots (1980)
Fuel Oil	110 gallons (95%)
Complement	3 (1980)
	250-gallon/minute fire pump.

32 FOOT PORTS AND WATERWAYS BOAT (PWB)

Builder Willard Marine in Oceanside CA
Number 32301 through 32356 Completed: 1976
Cost $102,000

Displacement	19,000 (lbs)
Length	33' 4" Beam: 11' 9" max
Main Engines	2 Caterpillar diesels BHP: 406
Performance	Max Speed: 20.4 knots (1980)
Fuel Oil	200 gallons (95%)

32 FOOT TRANSPORTABLE PORT SECURITY BOAT (TPSB)

Builder Kvichak Marine Industries Fairhaven, WA
52 in operation 2012

The boats can be transported by plane, or by vehicle with a trailer

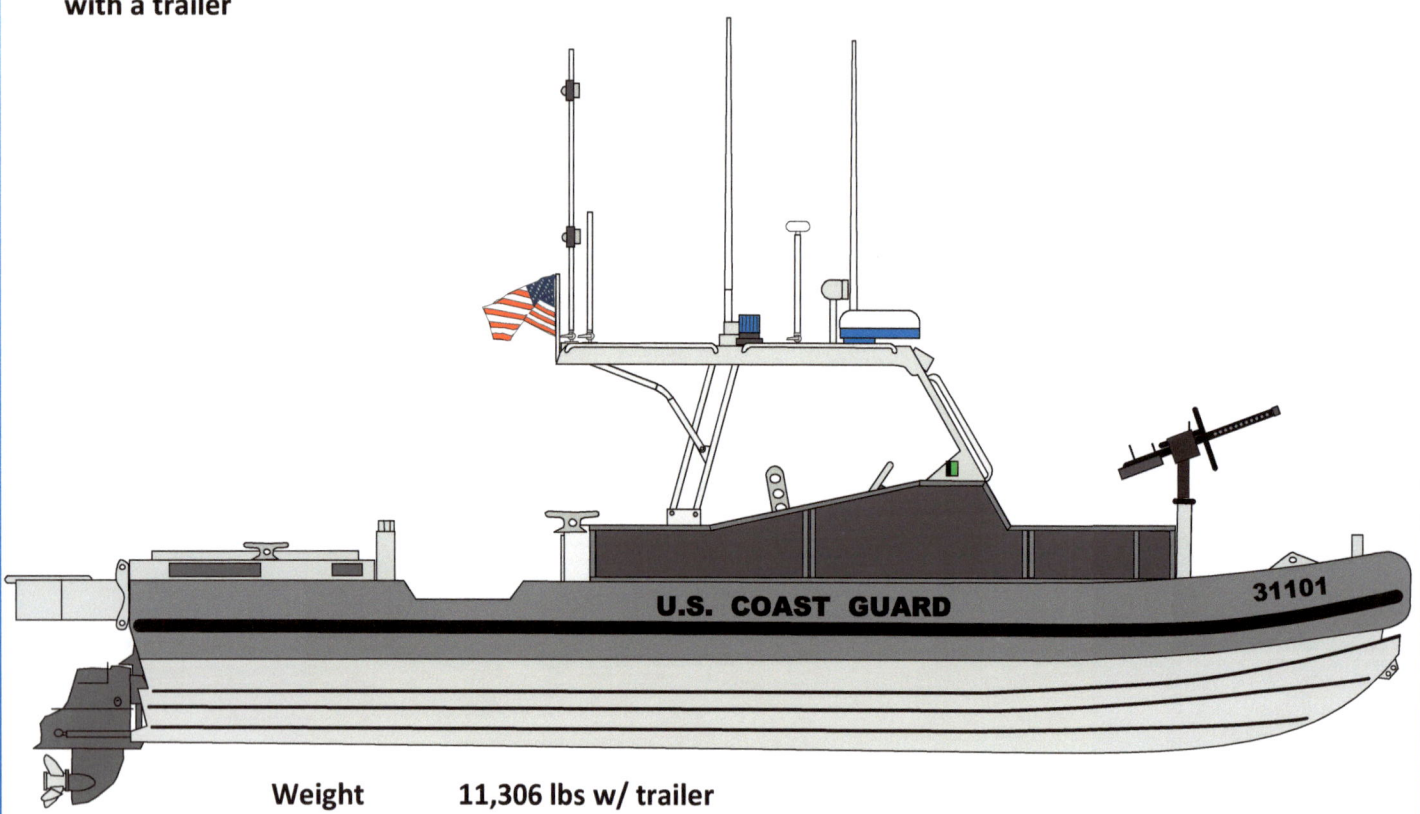

Weight	11,306 lbs w/ trailer
Length	32 ft 8 in Beam 8 ft 6 in Draft 1'9"
Propulsion	Two (2) 315hp Yanmar diesel inboard engines w/ Mercury outdrives
Fuel Capacity	150 Gallons
Speed	40-45 knots
Endurance	8 hrs idle speed and 2 hrs full speed
Crew	4
Armament	2 x M2HB .50-caliber machine guns, 2 x M240B machine guns Anti-Swimmer grenades, Small arms, Armour Ballistic panels
Towing Capacity	5 tons

18 FOOT ICE RESCUE TRANSPORT (SPC-IRT)

Builder American airboat corp Orange, TX

18-to-23 foot airboat special purpose craft - Primary mission is ice search and rescue and shallow water or flood operations.

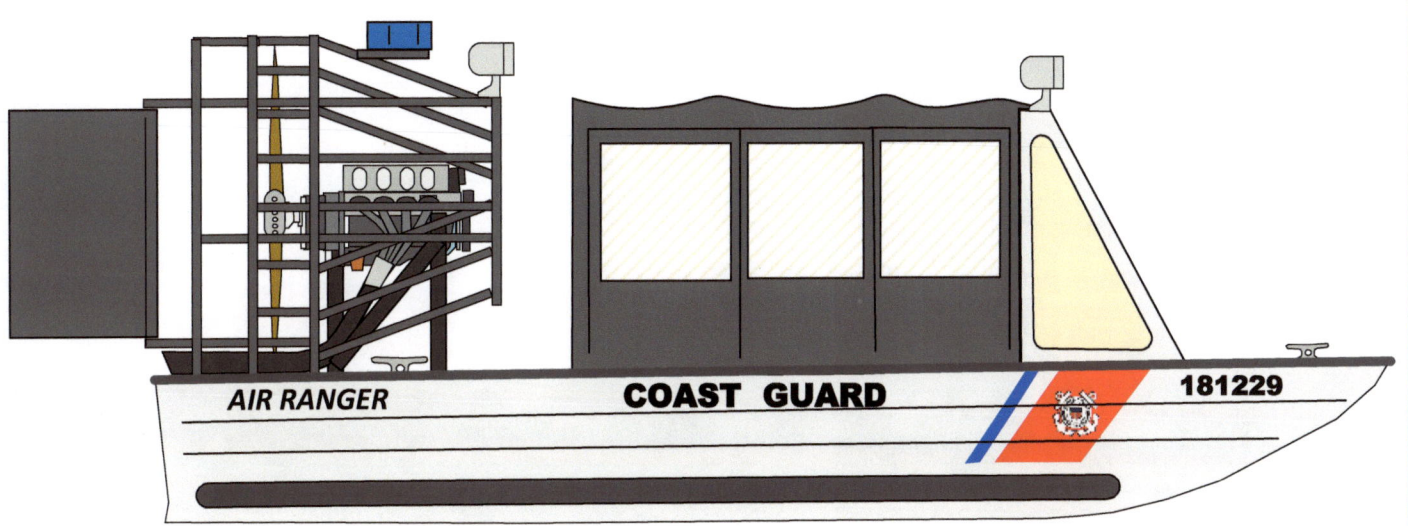

Length	18 ft – 20 ft
Power	Marine Power 556HP Engine

Side By Side Operator Seating
6 Inch Walkarounds
Driving Light Rail
4ft Rudders
3/8" Poly On Bottom And Sides

21 FOOT ICE RESCUE TRANSPORT (SPC-IRT)

Built by Dynamarine Performance Boats Topeka, KS

18 to 23 foot airboat special purpose craft - Primary mission is ice search and rescue and shallow water or flood operations.

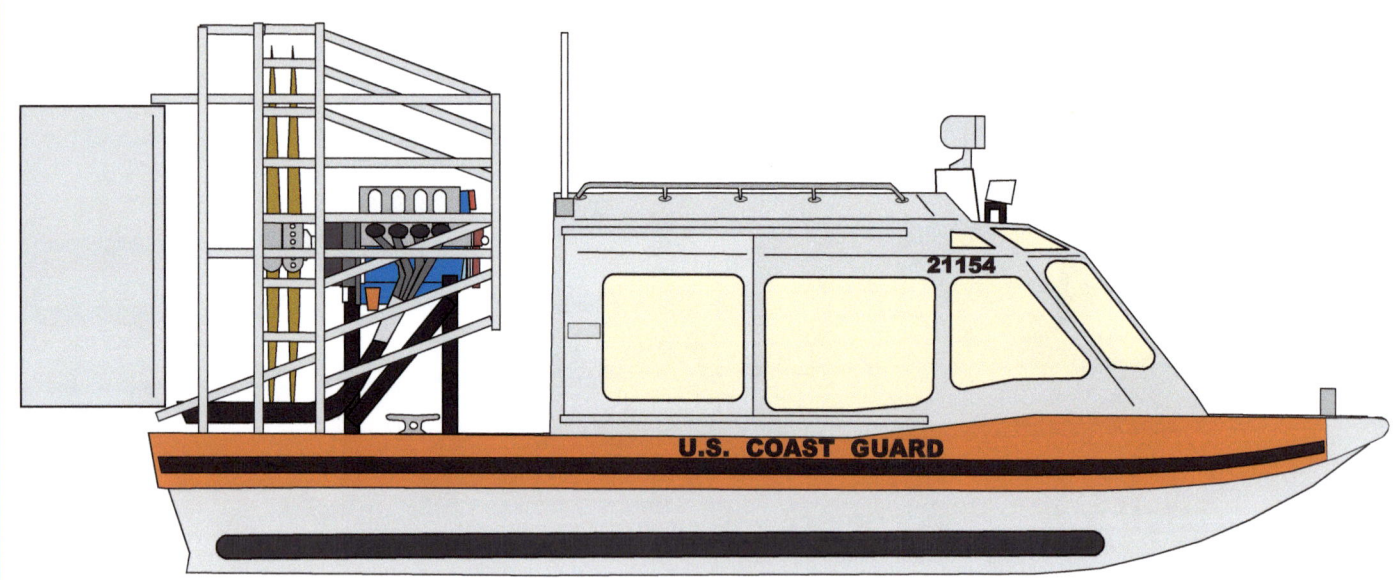

Weight	(full fuel): 5000lbs
Length	22' Beam: 8'6
Fuel capacity	58 gal
Engine	825hp LT5
Drive	Ballistic Counter Rotator
Props	82" JX/JR
Seating capacity	6

24 FOOT SPECIAL PURPOSE CRAFT - SHALLOW WATER PATROL CRAFT (SPC-SW)

Builder Metal Shark, Jeanerette, Louisiana
#24500-24590

Displacement	7,800lb in fully loaded condition
Length	25' 8'6" beam 1'6" draft
Power	Twin 150HP gasoline outboard engines
fuel	100gal
Speed	45kts max 30kts cruise
Range	225nm at cruise
Operating distance	from shore is 5nm
Hoist weight	3300lbs

capable of mounting one machine gun in forward cockpit

25 FOOT DEFENDER RB-HS (A CLASS)

A Class   Search and rescue, Security Response Team (MSRT)
B Class   Search and rescue, law enforcement
C Class   Port Security Units

Builders   A class   SAFE Boats International
            B and C Class   Metal Shark Boats

Completed   over 700 all classes

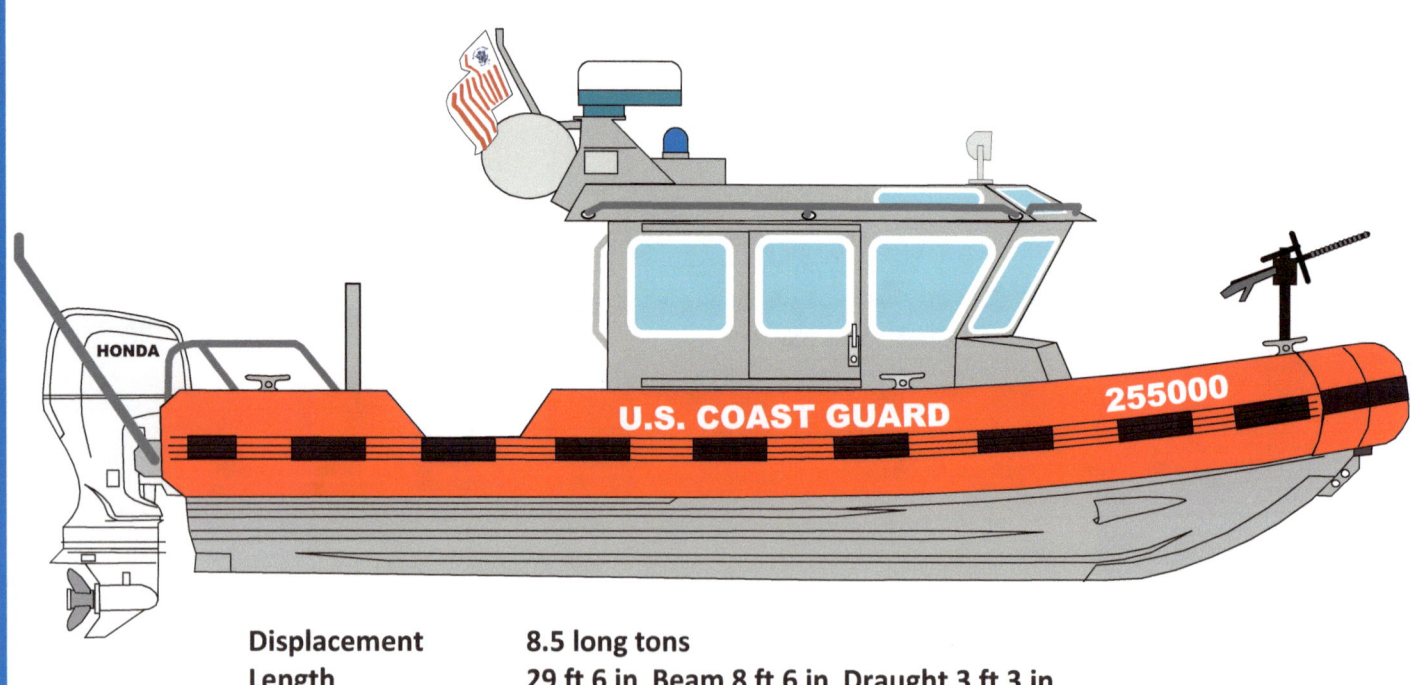

Displacement   8.5 long tons
Length   29 ft 6 in Beam 8 ft 6 in Draught 3 ft 3 in
Propulsion   2 × Honda 4-stroke outboard engines, 225 hp (168 kW) each
Speed   46 knots max 35 knots cruising
Range   150 nm
Complement   4 crew, 6 passengers
Armament   1 × M2HB, 2 × M240B M60 machine gun

27 FOOT PRESIDENTIAL SECURITY (PSD)

Built 1973 Magnum Marine Miami FL
Numbered 1,2,3,4,5

Stationed USCG Base Miami Beach FL

These specially purchased boats were used for the presidential security detail around President Richard Nixon's home on Key Biscayne during his many visits to the Miami area during his presidency.

Displacement 5,000 lbs
Length   27' beam 7'10"
Fuel capacity 130 gal
Top speed   73.8 knots
Power   twin Holman-Moody Ford engines
Drives   Mercury

27 FOOT SPECIAL PURPOSE CRAFT SHALLOW WATER II (SPC-SW)

Builder   Recondcraft, Estacada, OR.

Total built   49 2019-2023
Numbered   27101-27149

In service 2019 - Current

Length   27"
Beam   8' 6"
Draft   1'2"
Main Engines   350 HP Yanmar (1) EPA Tier 3 compliant
Speed   35+ mph
Range   150 NM at 30 kts
Complement   3

29 FOOT RESPONSE BOAT SMALL (RB-S II)

Builder   Metal Shark
Built   470 total
Cost $150 million

In service 2012 - Current

Displacement   8,300 pounds
Length   28 ft 8 in Beam 8 ft 5 in Draft 1 ft 8 in
Propulsion   Twin Honda 225 HP outboards
Speed   40+ knots
Range   150 nautical miles
Max towing   10 displacement tons
Armament   2 x M240B machine guns Small arms Ballistic panels installed in the cabin

Max operating seas: 6 feet with no surf or breaking seas

30 FOOT UTILITY BOAT MEDIUM MARK 1 (UTB)

Most 30 ft UTB's were built by the Coast Guard's Curtis Bay Yard over the period 1954 to 1983, with the Mark III version boats built by the Pearson Corp Bristol, RI.

Mark I built of steel
Mark II built of plywood
Mark III built of fiberglass

Built by Coast Guard yard, Curtis bay, MD
Cost 36,392,00 1957

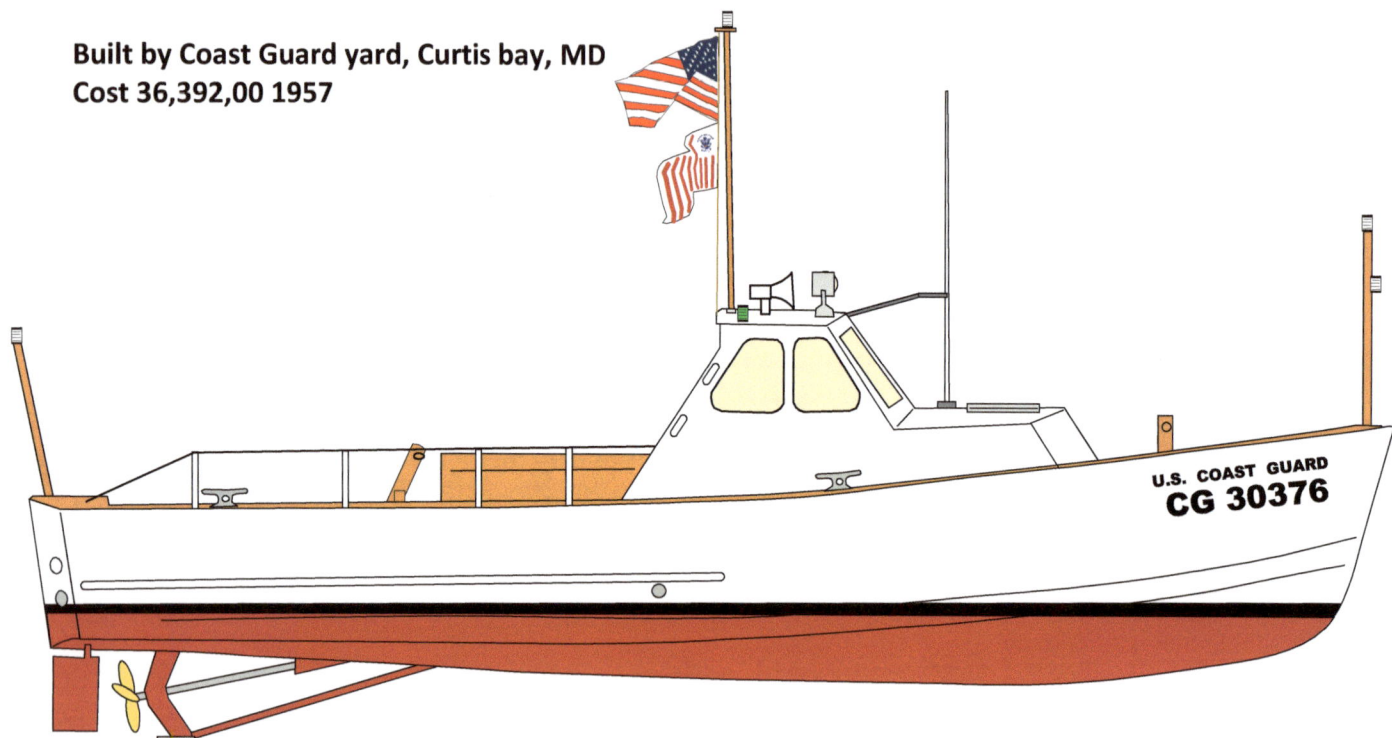

Displacement	10,464 full load
length	30 ft. 8ft. 9in. beam draft 2 ft 9 in.
Propulsion	single diesel engine with single propeller
Speed	28 mph max 22 cruise
Fuel	120gal
Range	220 mi at 22 mph
Capacity	3 crew 18 total

30 FOOT NON STANDARD BOAT (NSB)

Builder Formula yachts Miami FL

Seized by U.S. government for drug smuggling. Transferred to U.S. Coast Guard.

Stationed at Base Miami Beach fl during the 1980's

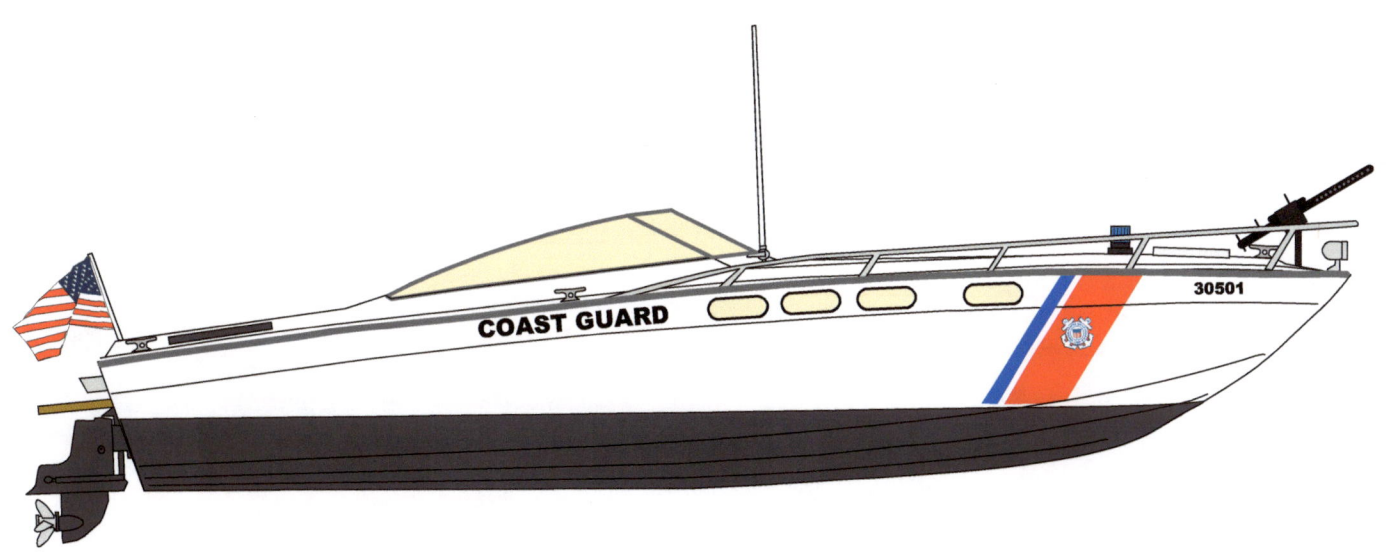

Net Weight	6950 lbs.
Length	30'
Beam	8'0"
Draft	2'10"
Engine	454 ci V8 (2) 330 hp
Fuel	115 gallons
Speed	50+ MPH
Complement	3

30 FOOT UTILITY BOAT MEDIUM (UTB)

Mark I built of steel Built by Coast Guard Yard Curtis Bay MD
Mark II built of plywood Built by Coast Guard Yard Curtis Bay MD
Mark III built of fiberglass Built BY Pearson Corp., Bristol, RI.

Cost 46,00.00 1968

30489 was modified for the Miami to Nassau offshore powerboat race and finished 5th out of 59 starters.

30564 was fitted with hydrofoils

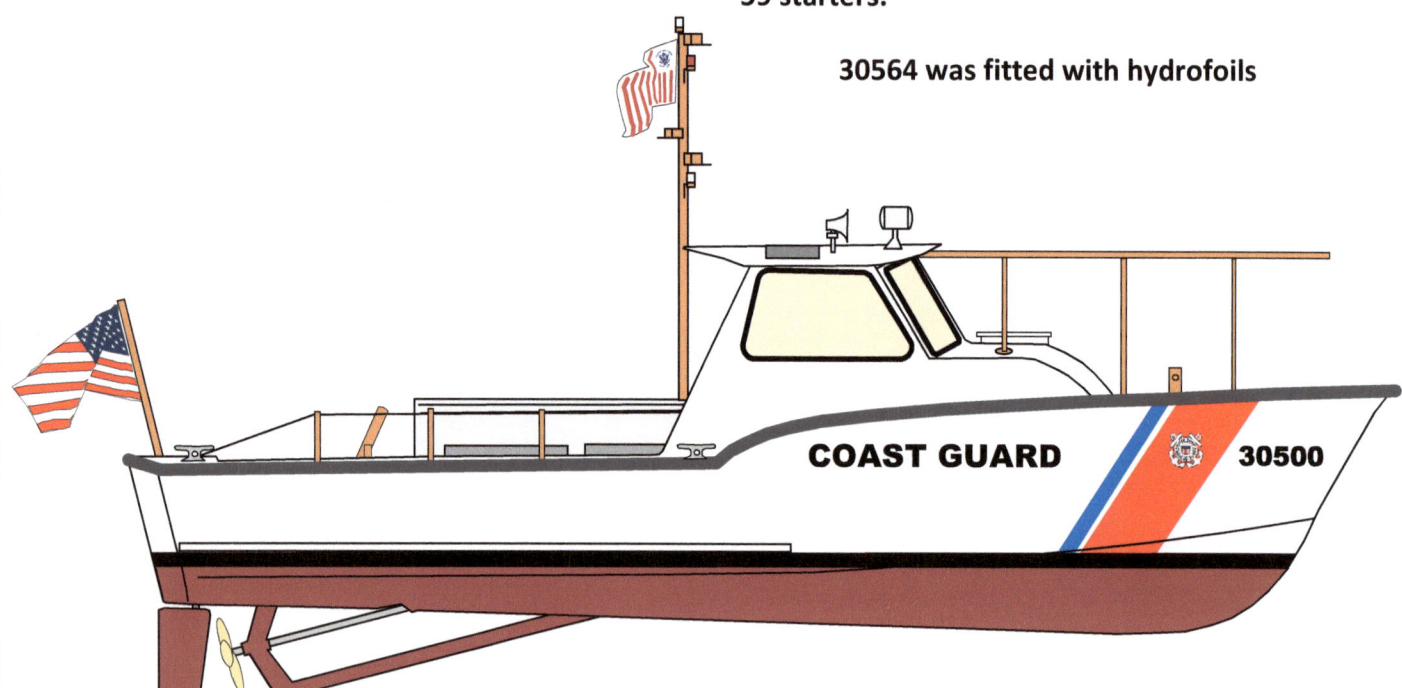

Displacement 13,500 lbs
Length 30' Beam 10'7" draft 3'
Fuel Capacity 112 (95%) gals
Top speed 25 kts
Range 170 nm
Power 1 cummins diesel HP 270-280
Complement 3

33 FOOT SPECIAL PURPOSE CRAFT LAW ENFORCEMENT (SPCLE)

Builder Safe boats

Contracted and paid by the Navy for the Coast Guard

110 boats

Displacement 11,960 pounds
Length 35.4 feet Beam: 10 feet Draft: 30 inches
Power three Mercury Verado 275hp outboard motors
Speed 60+ knots
Range 250 nautical miles
Crew 6

a zero to plane time under three seconds, and a top speed of more than 60 miles per hour

In service 2005 - Current

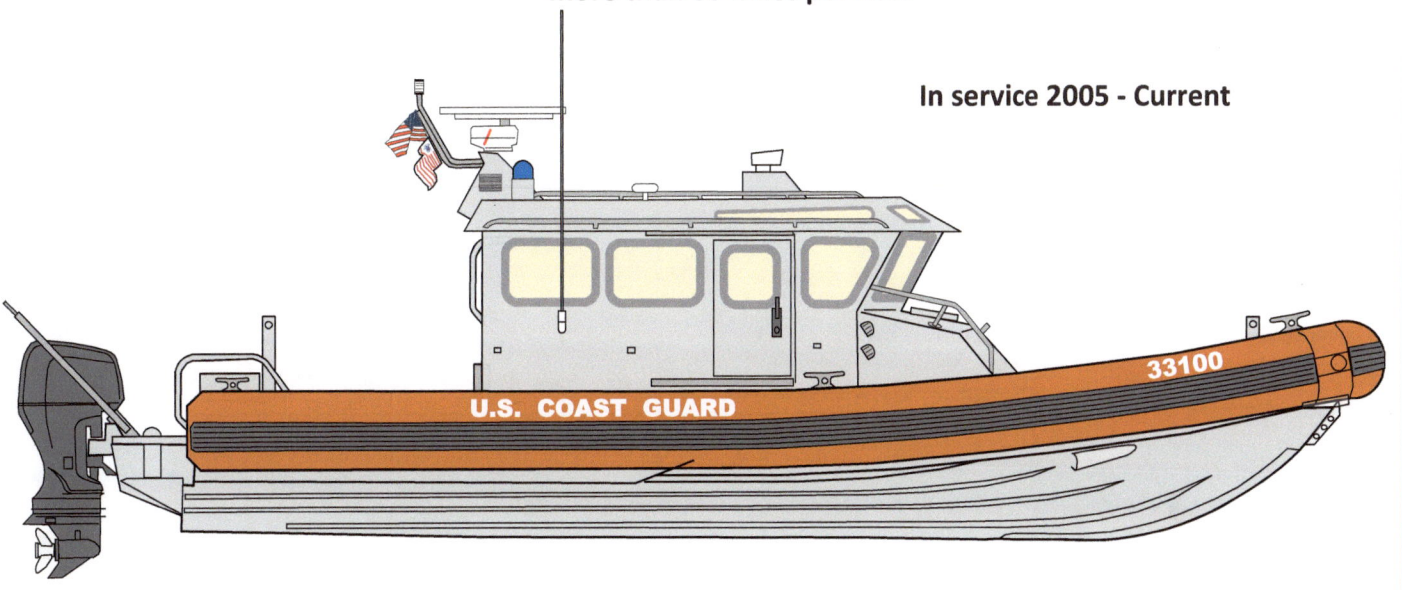

A new, high-speed boat to interdict smugglers' "go-fast" craft, the SPCLE is derived from the proven U.S. Department of Homeland Security 33-foot Defender-class boats. The fully enclosed heated and air-conditioned cabin, with as many as six shock mitigating seats, reduces crew fatigue and allows operations in heavier seas. With a forward gunner's station, increased operational range, a zero to plane time under three seconds, and a top speed of more than 60 miles per hour the 33-foot SPCLE is an ideal law enforcement platform.

35 FOOT LAND AMPHIBIOUS RESCUE CRAFT (LARC)

Builder   LeTourneau-Westinghouse, Longview Tx
Cost   47,850
Completed   1963 thru 1967
Numbered   35086 thru 35100; 35112 thru 35113; 35738 & 35747

Stationed between Massachusetts and North Carolina.

Removed from service between 1968 & 1979

Displacement	20,063 lbs
Length	35'
Beam	10'
Main Engines	1 diesel 300 hp
Performance	max speed on land, 30 mph 8 knots in the water
Range	10 hours at 18 mph on land
Complement	3

38 FOOT AIR CUSHION VEHICLE (ACV)

Builders	British Hovercraft Corporation
	Bell Aerosystems
Built	1965
Cost	$1 million

Transferred from the Navy
3 in CG service 1970 to 1975

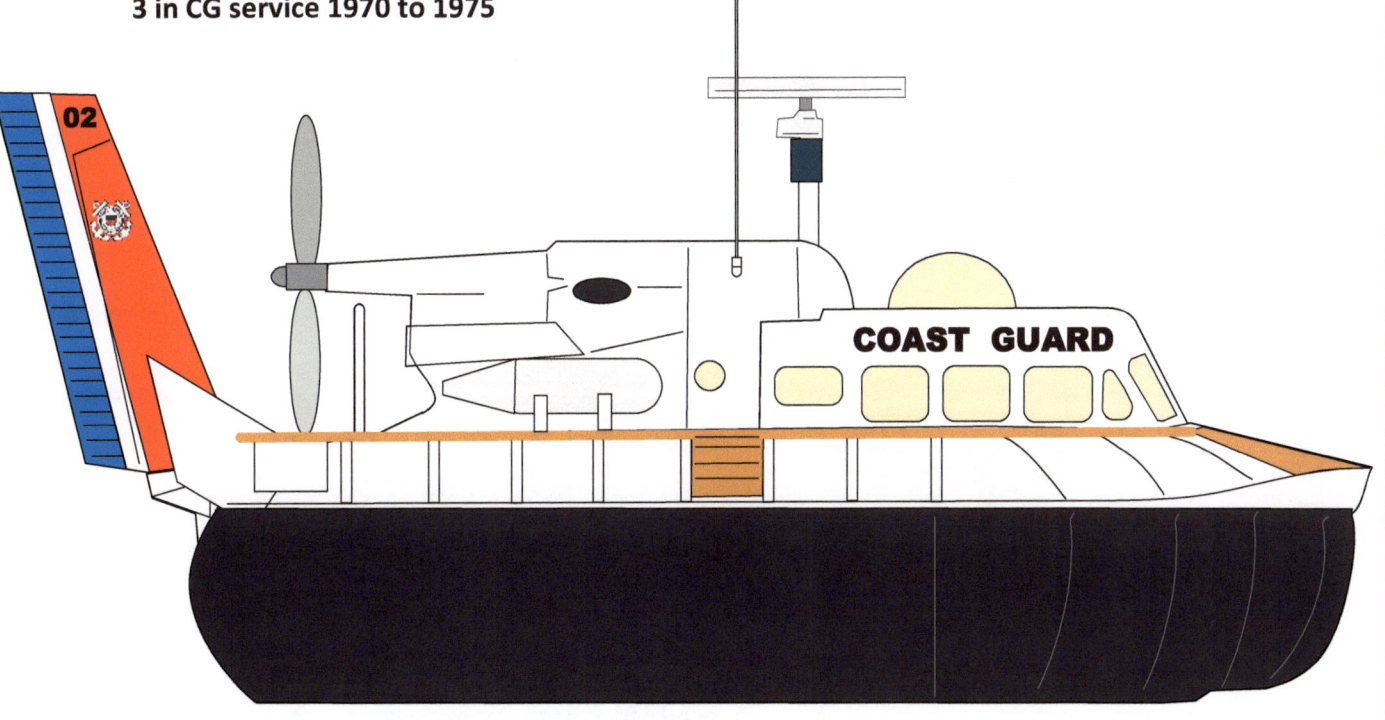

Tonnage	15,660 pounds
Length	38 feet 10 inches Beam 23 feet 9 inches
Height	16.5 feet on cushion
Propulsion	GE 7LM100-PJ102 gas turbine 900 horsepower
Speed	70 knots
Range	300 nautical miles
Endurance	7 hours
Crew	3

38 FOOT SPECIAL PURPOSE CRAFT TRAINING BOAT (SPC-TB)

Builder Metal Shark Jeanerette, LA
Total built 16

38-foot training boat special purpose craft - The 38-foot training boat special purpose crafts are intended to operate at Coast Guard Training Center Yorktown as a platform to teach the basics of seamanship and boat handling during Boatswain's Mate "A" school

In service 2010 - Current

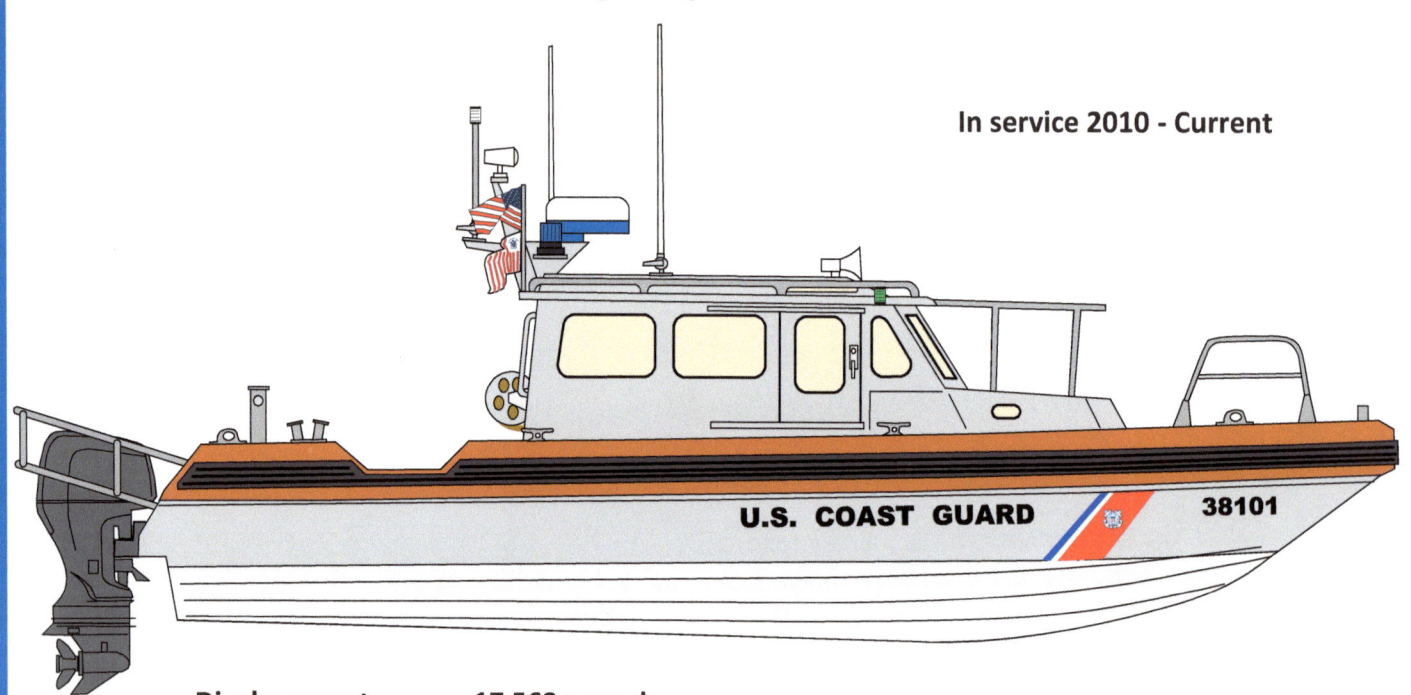

Displacement	17,563 pounds
Length	40'-9" Beam Overall 10'-8 3/4" Operational Draft 3'-0 3/4"
Propulsion	Two Mercury Marine Verado 300 HP5, 4-stroke outboard engines
Generator	Westerbeke diesel generator 11.5 KW
Fuel Tank Capacities	400 gallons: gas 28 gallons: diesel
Speed	38 knots max @ 5500 RPM Cruise Speed 24 knots @ 4500 RPM
Max Range	260 nm at cruise
Maximum Distance from Shore	50 NM
Capacity	2 crew, 6 students

40 FOOT UTILITY BOAT LARGE MARK IV (UTB)

Mark I, II, IV, VI
built by Coast Guard Yard Curtis Bay, MD

Mark III built by Universal Molded Fiberglass

Mark V built by W.R. Chance and Associates of Waldorf, MD

Cost $47,675 (Mark I 1951) $62,189 (Mark IV 1959)

Numbered 40369-40609 Total Built: 236

Completed 8 September 1950 through 16 May 1966

Displacement 23,765 lbs
Length   40' Beam 11' 2" Draft 3' 2" max
Main Engines 2 GMC 6-71 diesels (190 HP each)
Performance   Max Speed 22 knots (1951)
              Cruising Speed 15 knots
Range   190-mile
Fuel Oil   228 gallons (1951); 370 gallons (1953)
Complement 3

40 FOOT UTILITY BOAT LARGE MARK VI (UTB)

Built 1   Mark V Prototype Plastic Single Screw   40043
       7   Mark V Mod 1 Plastic Single Screw   40590-40596
       13 Mark VI Plastic Twin Screw   40597-40609

Mark I, II, IV, VI
built by Coast Guard Yard Curtis Bay, MD

Mark III built by Universal Molded Fiberglass

Mark V built by W.R. Chance and Associates of Waldorf, MD

Displacement   23,765 lbs
Length   40' Beam 11' 2" Draft 3' 2"
Power   twin Cummins V-6 Turbo-charged diesel engines producing 260 HP @3000 RPM
Speed   25 knots
Range   200 miles

41 FOOT UTILITY BOAT LARGE (UTB)

Builder   CG Yard, Curtis Bay, MD
Number   41300 through 41507
Completed   207 between 1972 to 1981
Cost $235,000

In service 1973 - 2014

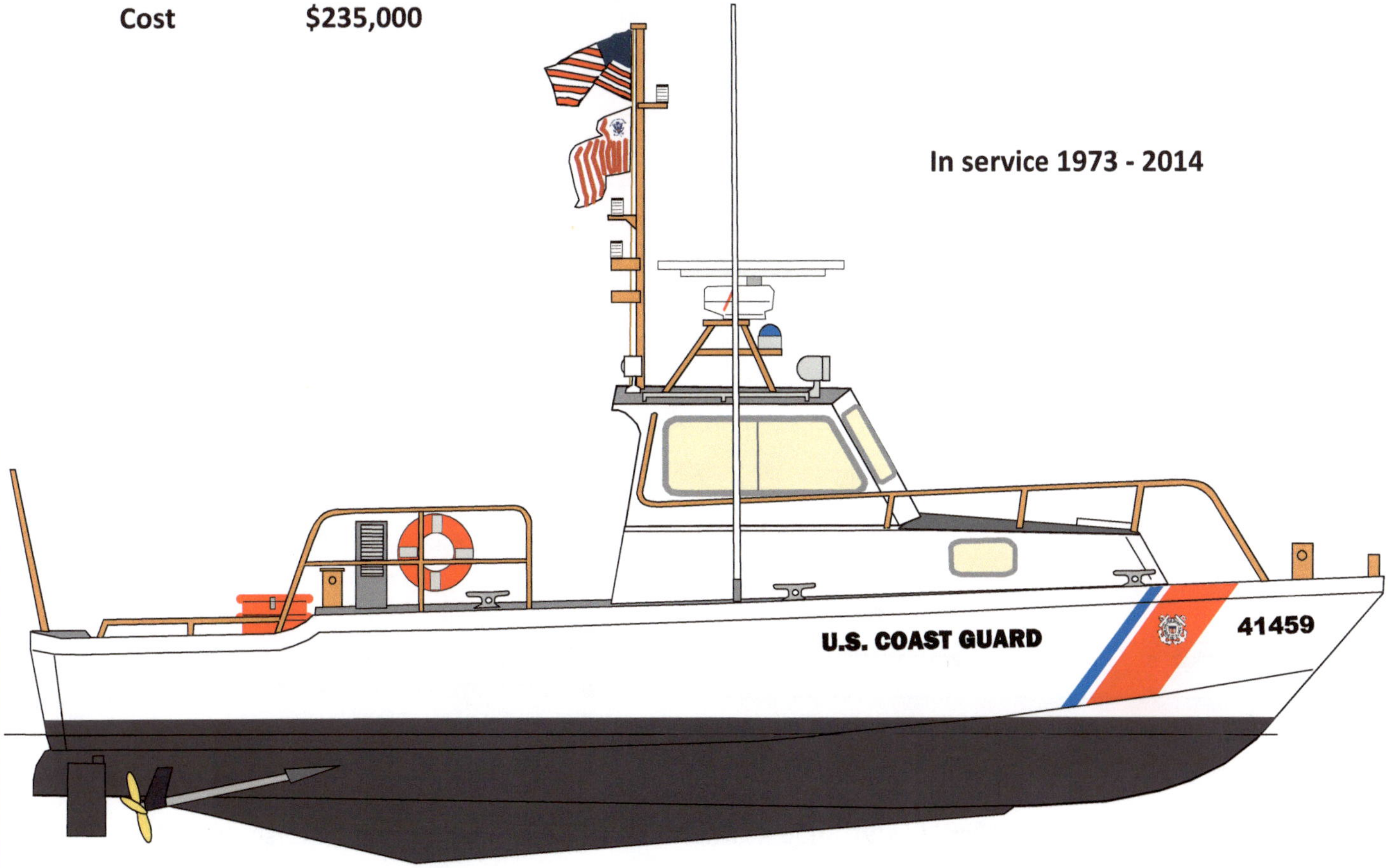

Displacement	28,500 lbs
Length	40'8" Beam: 13'6" Draft: 4'2"
Main Engines	2 Cummins diesels BHP: 560
Performance	Max Speed 26 knots
Range at cruise	sea state 0 - 300 nm
Fuel Oil	480 gallons (95%)
Complement	3

43 FOOT FAST COASTAL INTERCEPTOR (FCI)

The 43-foot FCI was designed and constructed by Tempest Marine for the USCG. The craft is based upon a 25-degree V-bottom monohull, designed and developed to be a large offshore boat capable of operating in heavy seas at high speeds.

Number   43501 through 43505
Completed   April 1987

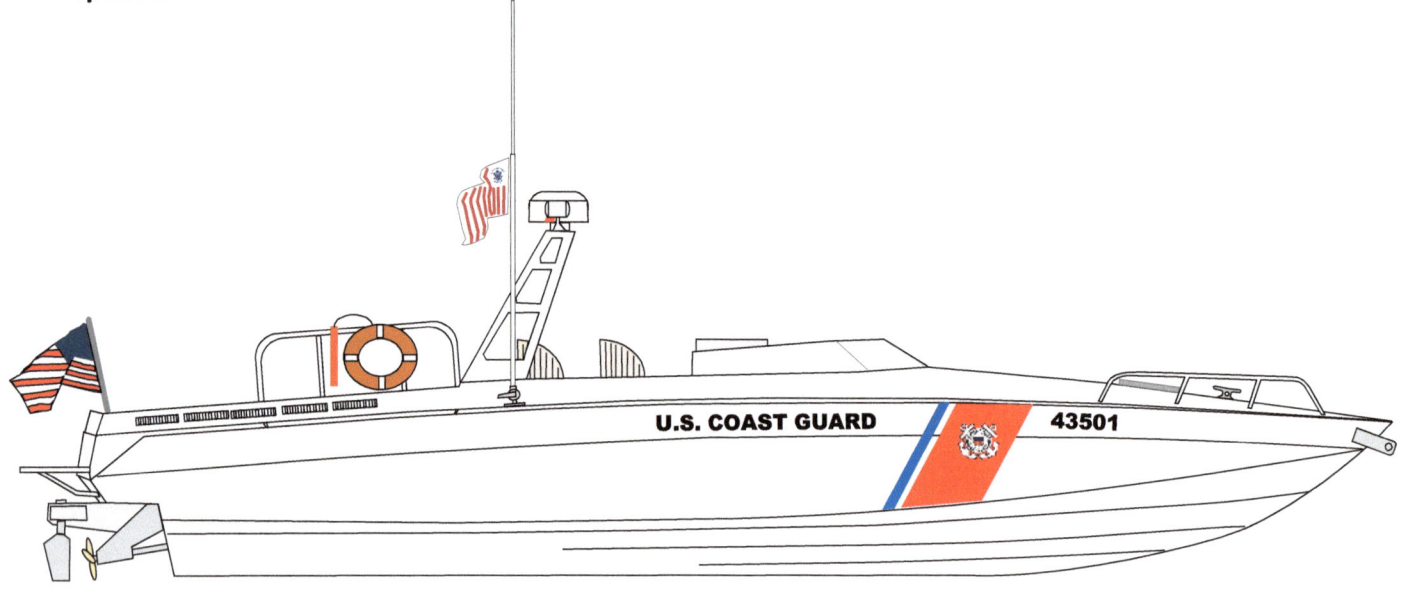

Used primarily for LE, stationed at Miami Beach, Fort Lauderdale, and Islamorada

Length	43' 6" Beam: 9' 6" max Draft: 3' 3" max
Main Engines	2 Caterpillar diesels HP 750
Max Sustained	39+ knots
Diesel	340 gallons
Complement	4-6

45 FOOT RESPONSE BOAT MEDIUM (RB-M)

Builder Marinette Marine Corporation and Kvichak Marine Industries
174 in service 45601 -45774

Maximum seas 10 feet
Maximum winds 30 knots
Maximum towing capacity: 100 tons
Operation in ice Light surface ice and slush at idle speed

In service 2008 - Current

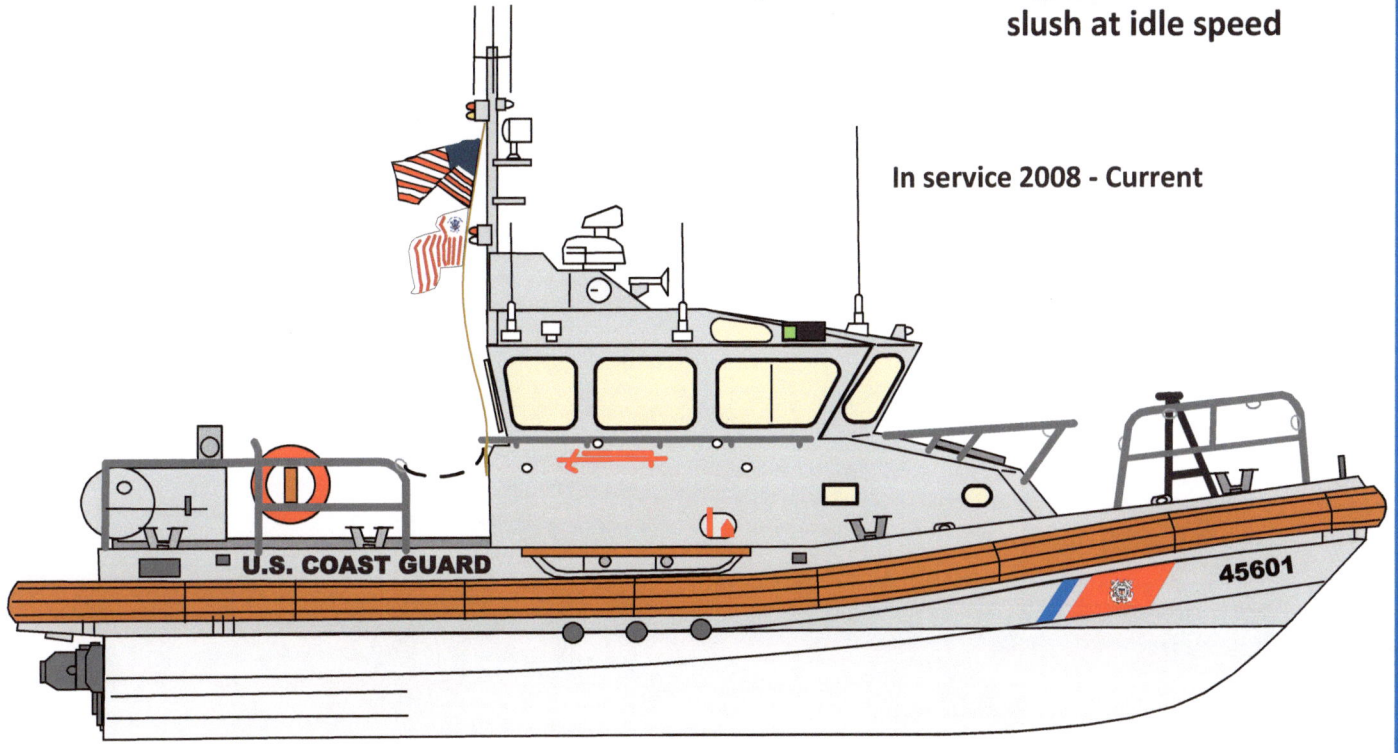

Displacement	16.3 ton
Length	44 ft 9 in Beam 14 ft 7.75 in Draft 3 ft 4 in
Power	2 × MTU Detroit Diesel turbocharged Series 60 engines, 825 hp total
Propulsion	2 × Rolls-Royce FF-Series waterjets
Speed	30 knots (cruise) 42.5 knots (max)
Range	250 nm at 30 knots
Complement	4
Armament	2 × M240B general-purpose machine guns

64 FOOT MOTOR SPECIAL PURPOSE CRAFT (SPC-SV)

Builder: Gladding-Hearn Shipbuilding, Somerset, Ma
Construction: Aluminum
12 vessels built

The 64-foot screening vessel is designed to perform mission activities in adverse weather and sea conditions. missions include port, waterways and coastal security, search and rescue and law enforcement.

In service 2009 - Current

Length Overall	64' - 11" Beam: 19' - 0" Draft: 3' - 8"
Power	1,300 HP x 2
Speed	In excess of 30 kts
Fuel Capacity	1,400 gallons
Water Capacity	42 gallons

In the 1920's, during Prohibition, the Coast Guard fleet expanded to over 320 cutters and destroyers, and hundreds of smaller boats. The budget increased from $9.3 million to over $24 million in 1927 and personnel increased from 4,000 men to 10,000. Coast Guard crews manned U.S. Navy warships for the first time and extensively used radios and (RDF) radio direction finders.

After setting up temporary aviation operations at Squantum Naval Air Station, the first Coast Guard aviation interdiction took place a month later on June 24th 1925. This lead to the purchase of five new Coast Guard aircraft and the beginning of the Coast Guard Aviation branch.

ANB	**Aids to Navigation Boats**
BU	**Buoy Boat**
BUSL	**Buoy Boat, Stern Loading**
ANB	**Aids to Navigation Boat**
ANLB	**Aids to Navigation Logistics Boat**
TANB	**Trailered Aids to Navigation Boat**

Aides to navigation boats operate in harbors, bays and waterways throughout the United States. Generally speaking, they return to the station at the end of the day, but some have small crews quarters that allow them to extend deployments to a few days.

WLB	**Seagoing buoy tender**
WLI	**Inland buoy tenders**
WLIC	**Inland construction tenders**
WLM	**Coastal buoy tenders**
WLR	**River buoy tenders**
WLV	**Lightship**

Buoy tenders are generally some of the longest serving cutters in the Coast Guard. The seagoing class operate globally including resetting aids to navigation in Iraq during the conflict. Inland and river tenders operate either as a standalone cutter or pushing work barges 70 to 130 feet in length. The Coast Guard has approved a contact to replace the inland and river tenders with 16 new cutters in 2030. There were over 15 lightships serving in the 1970's with the most famous being the Nantucket I and II. These are the only lightships to receive official names.

21 FOOT TRAILERABLE ATON BOAT (TANB)

Builder   sealark marine 1974
Cost   8,800
Built   90 total

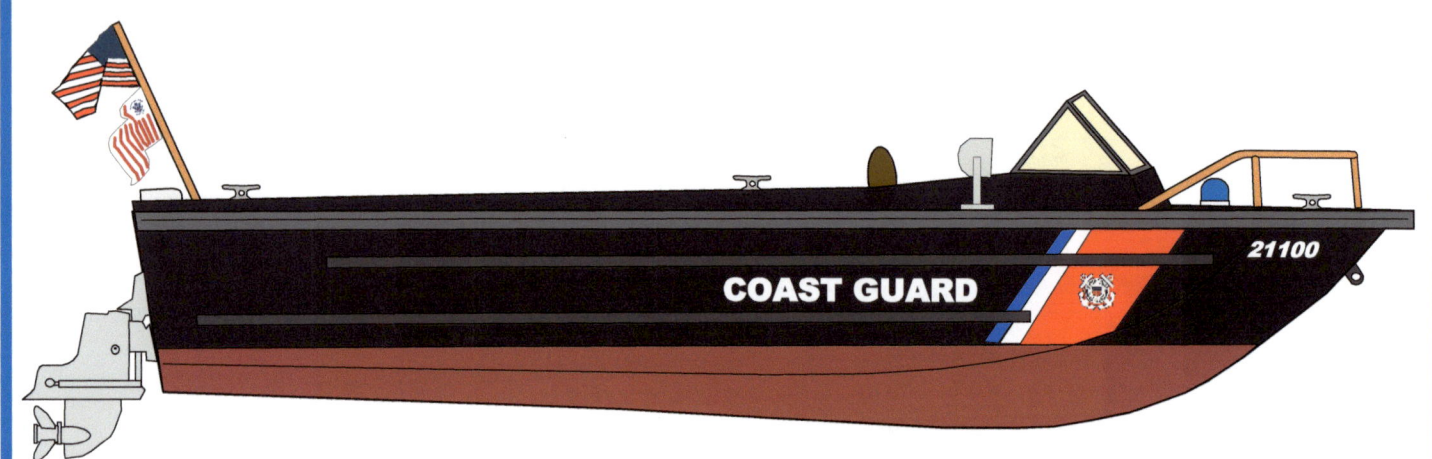

Displacement	4,080 lbs.
Length	21' 6-½" beam 7'6" draft 1'4"
Engine	165 hp mercruiser inboard / out drive
Speed	30 MPH max 21 mph cruise
Fuel capacity	36 gal
Range	at cruise 100 miles
Cargo Maximum	2,000 lbs.

26 FOOT TRAILERABLE AIDS TO NAVIGATION BOAT (TANB)

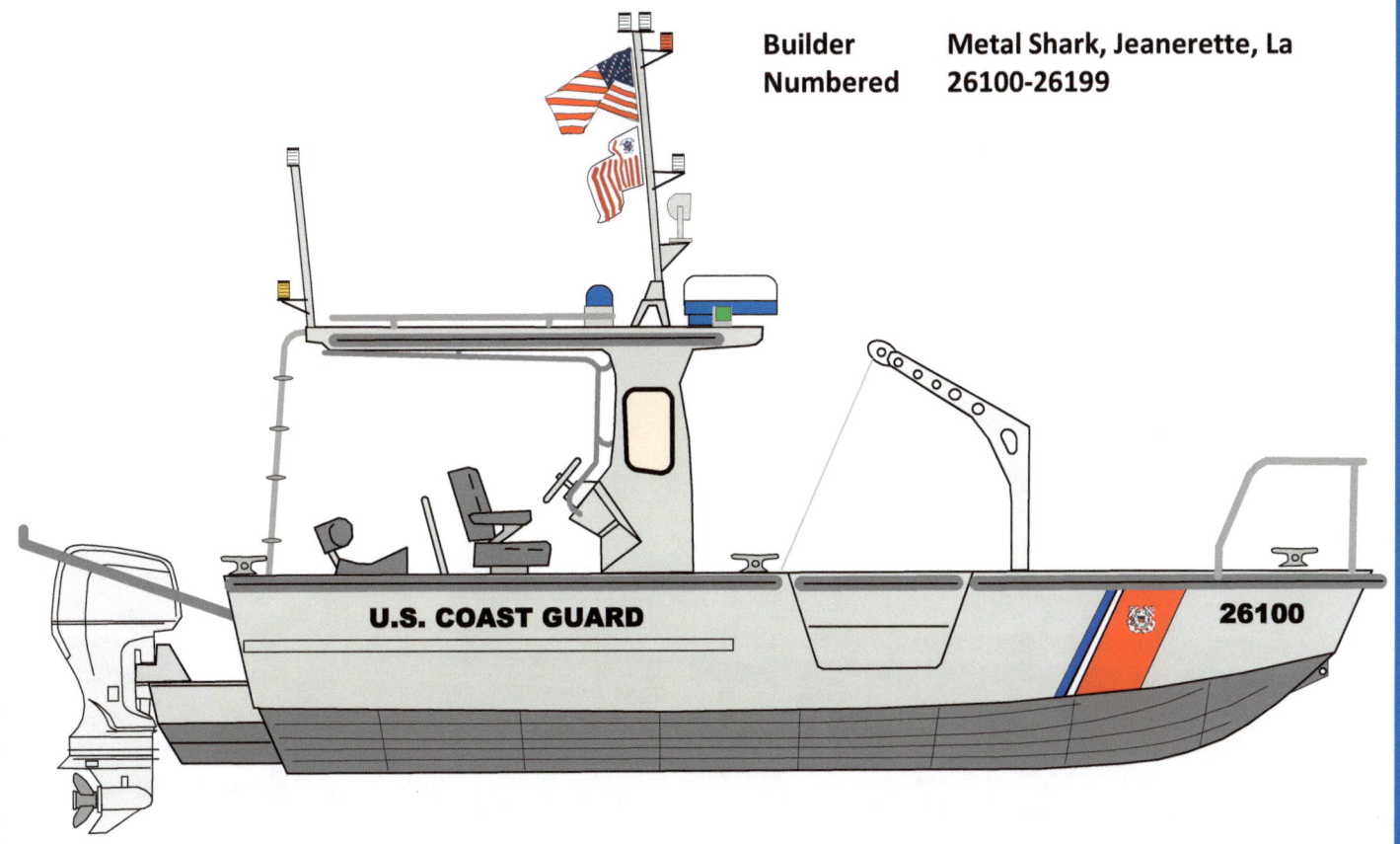

Builder   Metal Shark, Jeanerette, La
Numbered   26100-26199

Length	29 ft 7 in beam: 8 feet, draft: 2 ft 4 in
Engines	twin 150 hp 4-cycle outboard motors,
Speed	30 knots at 4,800 rpm
Range	170 nm at 4,800 rpm
Hoisting capacity	500 lb

Forward and stern-quarter weapons mounts capable of handling M240 machine guns. An additional recessed deck mount forward supports a tripod and .50 caliber machine gun.

45 FOOT BUOY BOAT (BU)

Builder	Coast Guard yard Curtis bay, MD
Number	45301 – 45316
Cost	132,625 (1959)

Displacement	68,000 lbs
Length	45' 4" Beam 15' 1" Draft 3'
Fuel Capacity	508 gals (95%)
Top speed	8.5 kts
Power	1 GM diesel 180 hp
Complement	4
Lift capacity	4,000 lbs

46 FOOT STERN LOADING BUOY BOAT (BUSL)

Builder	Hunt Shipyard
Cost	$154,000 1969
Numbers	46301-46306
Total	6

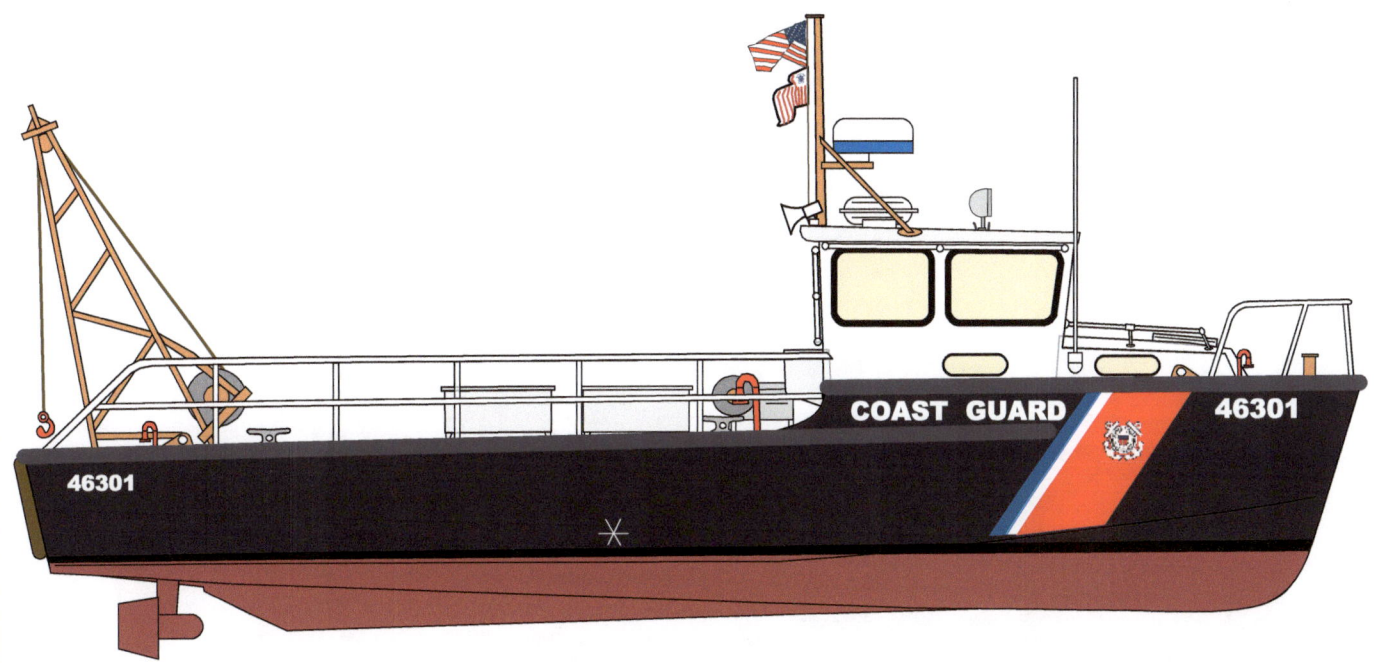

Displacement	43,500 lbs
Length	46'4" Beam 16'2" Draft 5'1"
Fuel	440 gal
Propulsion	diesel 6-71 180 hp steerable right-angle drive unit
Speed	9 kts max 8 kts cruise
Range	at cruise 440 miles
Lifting capacity	4,000 lbs
Cargo maximum	16,000 lbs

49 FOOT BUOY UTILITY STERN LOADING BOAT (BUSL)

Weight	71,690 lbs
Length	49' 2 Beam (Maximum): 16' 10" Draft 5' 6"
Propulsion	6CTA8.3M1 305 hp x2
Fuel	783 gallons
Speed	10.5 knots Cruise Speed 7 knots
Range	400 nm
Endurance	4 days
Maximum Seas	6 feet

In service 1997 - Current

Builder	Coast Guard yard Curtis bay MD
built	28 between 1997 to 2001
Numbered	49401-49428

Maximum Towing Capacity Bollard Pull: 11,000 lbs

55 FOOT AIDS TO NAVIGATION BOAT (ANB)

Builder	Derector shipyard Mamaroneck, NY
Completed	12
Cost	330,000 1975
numbered	55101 to 55112

500-gallon per minute fire pump

4-inch icebreaking capabilities

Displacement	68,620 lbs
Length	58' 0" beam 16' 9" draft 5' 2"
Engine	twin diesel hp 540 (each)
Fuel	1,045 gallons (95%)
Speed	22 kts max 14 kts cruise
Range	350 nm at 18 kts
Cargo capacity	4,000 lb
crane capacity	1,000 lb
Capacity	4 crew

56 FOOT CABLE LAYING LANDING CRAFT (LCM)

The Coast Guard operated several types of landing craft between 35 ft and 72 ft. The 36 ft LCVP was carried onboard icebreakers, the 56 ft LCM-6 and the 72 ft LCM-8 were used as cable laying craft to light houses and other duties.

Displacement	64 tons full load
Power plant	2 Detroit 6-71 diesel engines; 348 hp sustained; twin shaft
Length	56.2 feet Beam 14 feet
Speed	9 knots
Range	130 miles at 9 knots
Crew	5

65 FOOT INLAND BUOY TENDER (WLI)

Builder	Dubuque Boat & Boiler Company, Dubuque, IA
Built	3 1946 65303-65305
Builder	Reliable welding works, Olympic, WA
Built	2 1954 65400-65401

65400-65401

Displacement:	71 tons
Length:	65' Beam: 17' Draft: 4' 9" max
Machinery:	2 General Motors diesel, 400 hp, twin propeller
Fuel	914 gallons (95%)
Performance:	Max: 11.5 knots, 590 mile range Cruising: 10 knots, 720 mile range
Complement	8

65303-65305

68 tons
65' Beam: 17' Draft: 3' 6" max
1 General Motors diesel, 220 hp, single propeller
914 gallons (95%)
Max: 10 knots, 830 mile range
Cruising: 8 knots, 913 mile range
8

65 FOOT INLAND RIVER TENDER (WLR)

Builder	Plazer shipyard Houston TX	65 and 75 foot tenders push
	Gibbs corporation Jacksonville FL	68 to 130 foot barges
Built	6	
Cost	287,759.00 (1960)	

In service 1960 - Current

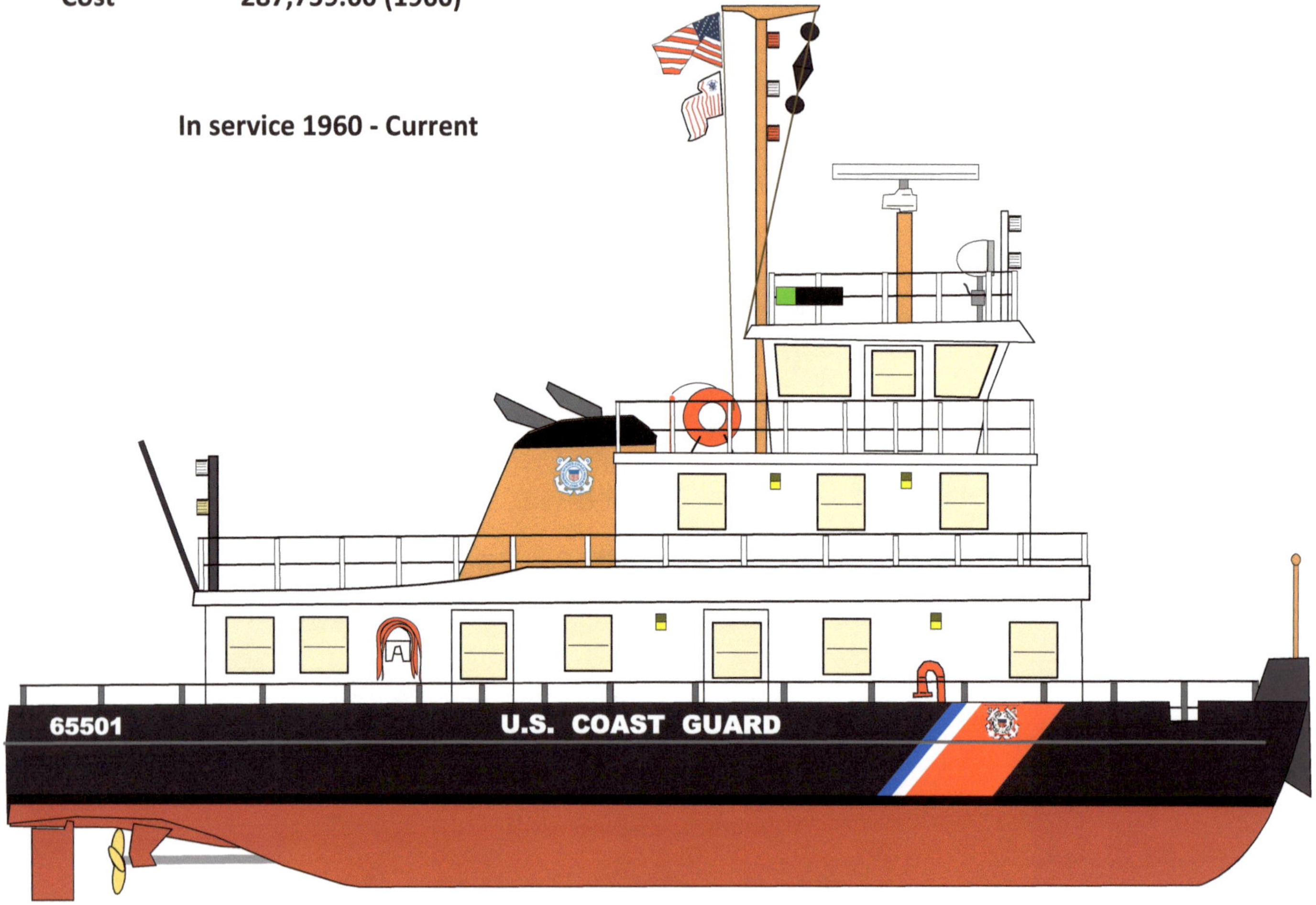

Length	65' 8" Beam 21' draft 5'
Engines	2 caterpillar diesels 600hp
Speed	12.5 kts max
Fuel	5,300 gal
Complement	16

128 FOOT AMBROSE CLASS LIGHTSHIP (WLV)

Builder   Coast Guard yard Curtis Bay, Md
Launched   4 August 1952

In service 1952 - 1985

WLV-612 and WLV-613 alternated at Nantucket Shoals as the Nantucket I and the Nantucket II, relieving each other approximately every 21 days.

During the 70's there were 21 lightships in operation

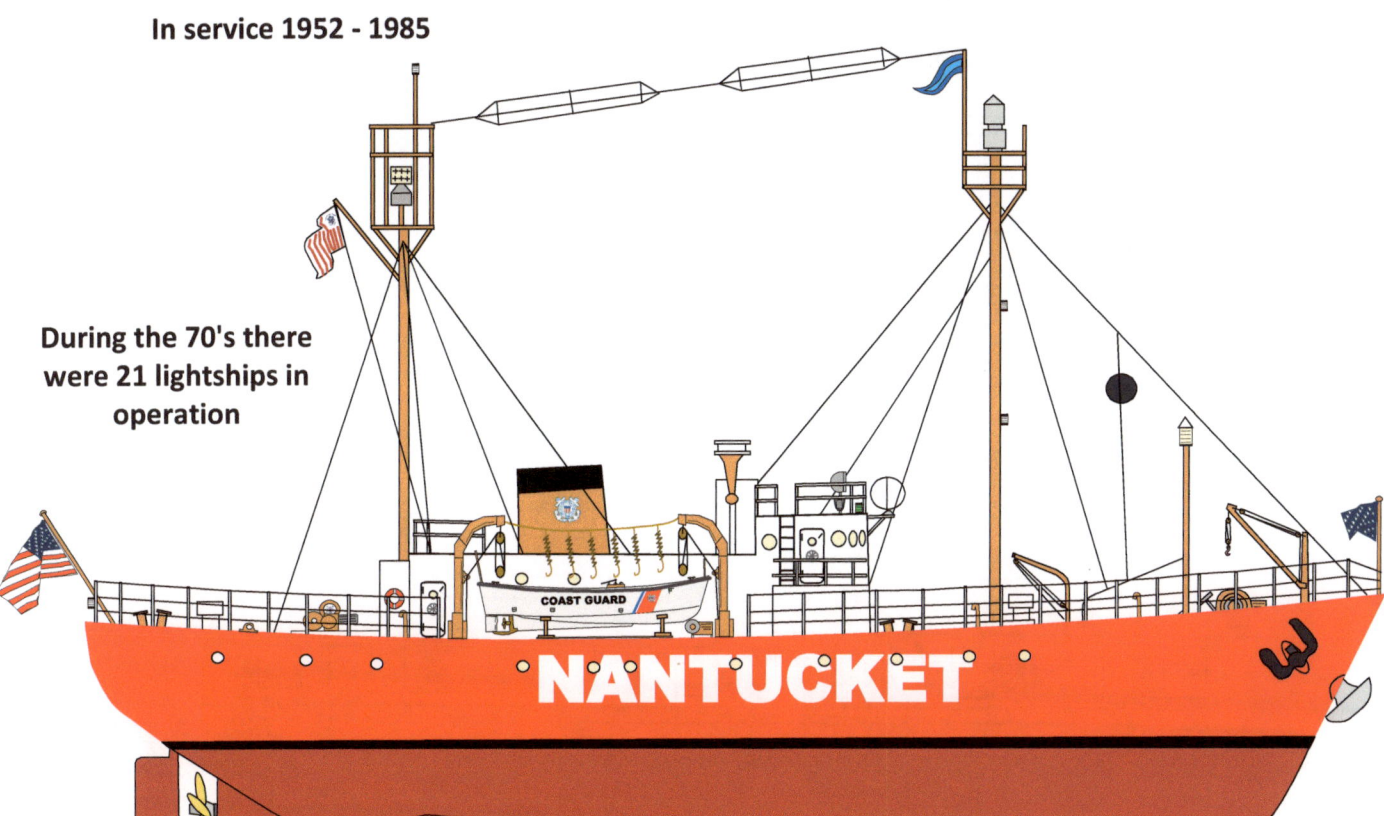

129 ft. class	WLV 604-605	Displacement	130 tons
128 ft. class	WLV 189, 196	Length	128 ft Beam 30 ft Draft 11 ft
115 ft. class	WLV 539	Propulsion	Detroit - Quad, 550 Hp
149 ft. class	WLV 534	Speed	9 knots
133 ft. class	WLV 523, 535, 536, 537, 538	Range	4000 miles
132 ft. class	WLV 528-533	Boats carried	26.6 ft. whale boat

75 FOOT INLAND CONSTRUCTION / BUOY TENDER

Builders   Gibs shipyard Jacksonville FL
Mc Dermott Fabricators Morgan city LA
Sturgeon Bay shipbuilding & dry dock co Sturgeon Bay WI
Dorchester Shipbuilding corp Dorchester NJ

75-Foot WLIC (1962-65)

65 and 75 foot tenders push 68 to 130 foot barges

Displacement	129 tons
length	76'1" ft beam 22'5" draft 4'6"
Power	2 Waukesha Motor corp
Speed	11.5 knots
Fuel	2,616 gallons
Ranger	1,300 nm
Complement	15

75-Foot Gasconade (C, D, E-Class) WLR (1964-70)

In service 1962 - Current

Length	75 ft beam 22 ft draft 5 feet 2 in
Power	2 IFM V1312ME Diesel Engines
Speed	10 knots
Range	3,000 nm
Complement	15

75-FOOT KANKAKEE CLASS RIVER BUOY TENDER (WLR)

75-Foot (F Class) WLR (1990-1991)

Builder Avondale Shipyard Small Boat Division, New Orleans, La

Numbered 75500 – 75501

Built 2

In service 1991 - Current

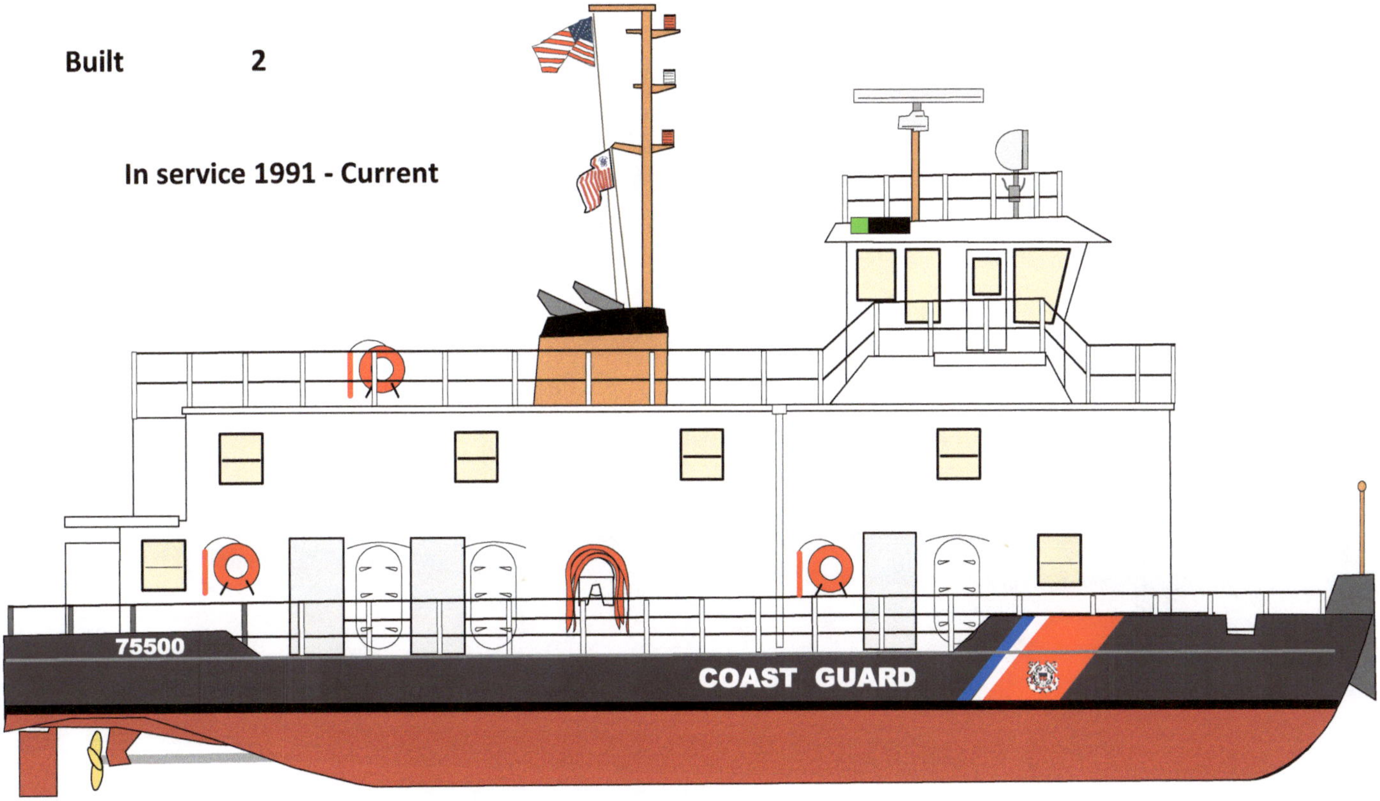

65 and 75 foot tenders push 68-to-130 foot barges

Displacement 172 tons
Length 75 ft Beam 24 ft Draft 5 ft
Propulsion 2 diesel engines turning 2 shafts with 1,080 bhp
Speed 12 knots
Range 8,000 nm
Lift 10,000 lbs
Crew 15

100 FOOT COSMOS-CLASS INLAND CONSTRUCTION TENDER (WAGL/WLIC)

Builder Dubuque Boat & Boiler Works, Dubuque, Iowa
Commissioned 1 November 1944
Cost $194,238.00

Reclassified
WLI (1966)
WLIC (1979)

WLIC 315 Smilax
Queen of the fleet status 2011

In service 1944 - Current

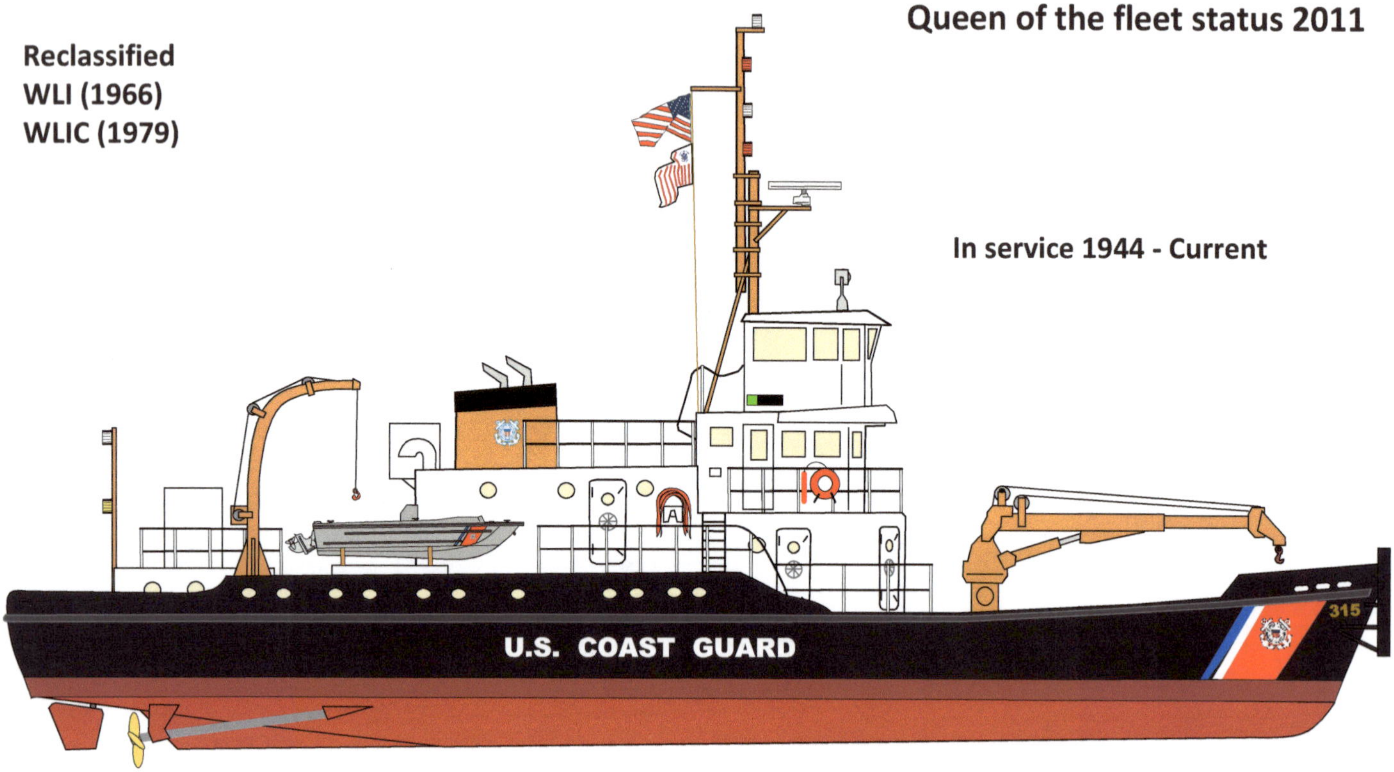

Displacement	175 long tons
Length	100 ft Beam 24.6 ft Draft 5.3 ft
Installed power	2 × Waukesha diesel engines 600 bhp
Speed	10.5 knots
Complement	16
Lift capacity	10,000 lbs
Length with barge	170 ft.
Can work without barge	

100 FOOT INLAND BUOY TENDER (WLI)

Builder Mobile ship repair inc. Mobile AL
Built 1964

Class "C"

In service 1964 - Current

Length	100' beam 24' Depth: 4'08"
Propulsion	2 Caterpiller diesel engines 2 propellers
Speed	10.6 knots max 9.4 knots cruise
Range	1,881 nm at cruise
Fuel	4,742 gal
Complement	1 warrant officer 13 crew (1964)
Boom capacity	5 tons

160 FOOT INLAND CONSTRUCTION TENDER (WLIC)

Builder　　　Coast Guard Yard Curtis bay, MD
Cost　　　　2,447,000 – 3,635,000 1974 – 1976
Bulit　　　　4

In service 1976 - Current

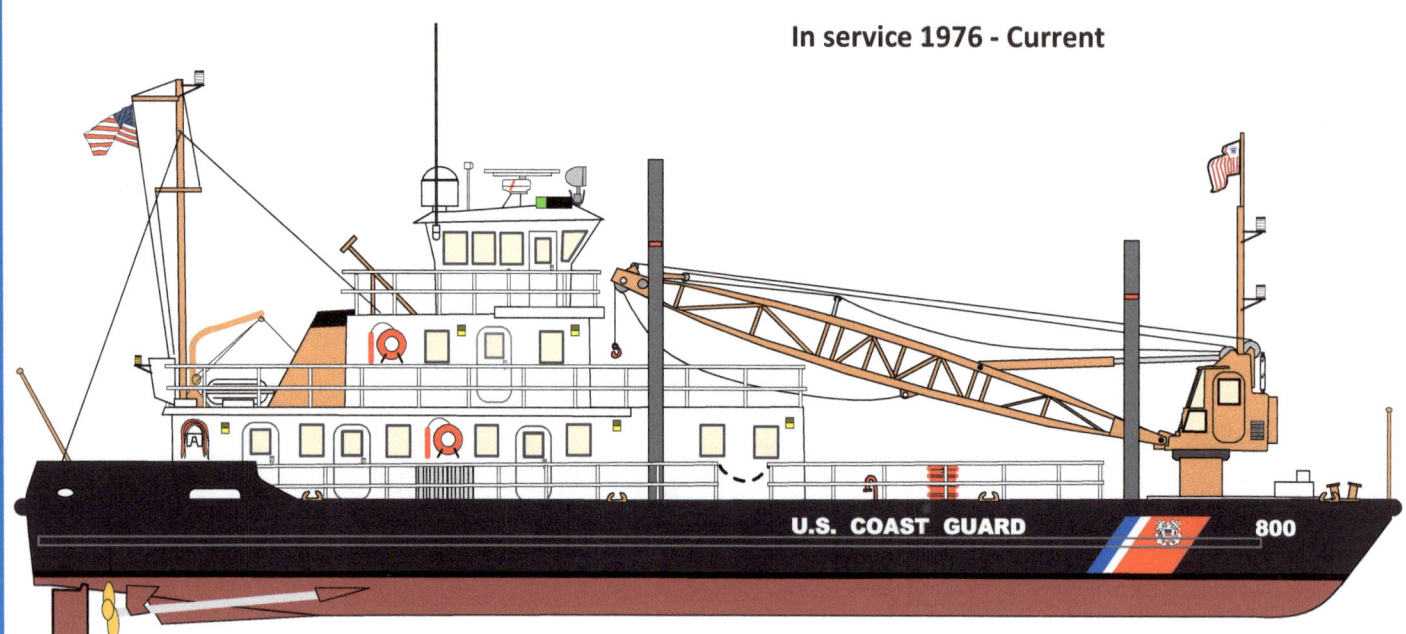

Displacement　459 tons
Length　　　　160' beam 30' max draft 3'10"
Engines　　　2 cummins diesels 1,000 hp total
Speed　　　　11 kts max 6.5 kts cruise
Range　　　　2,200 nm at 6.5 kts
　　　　　　　1,400 nm at 11 kts
Complement　15

133 FOOT WHITE-CLASS BUOY TENDER (WLM/WAGL)

Builders	For the Navy Niagara Shipbuilding Co. Basalt Rock Co. Erie Concrete & Steel Supply Co.	Numbered 540 to 547
Built	1944-1945 8 Transferred to US Coast Guard, 1946	

In service 1947 - 2002

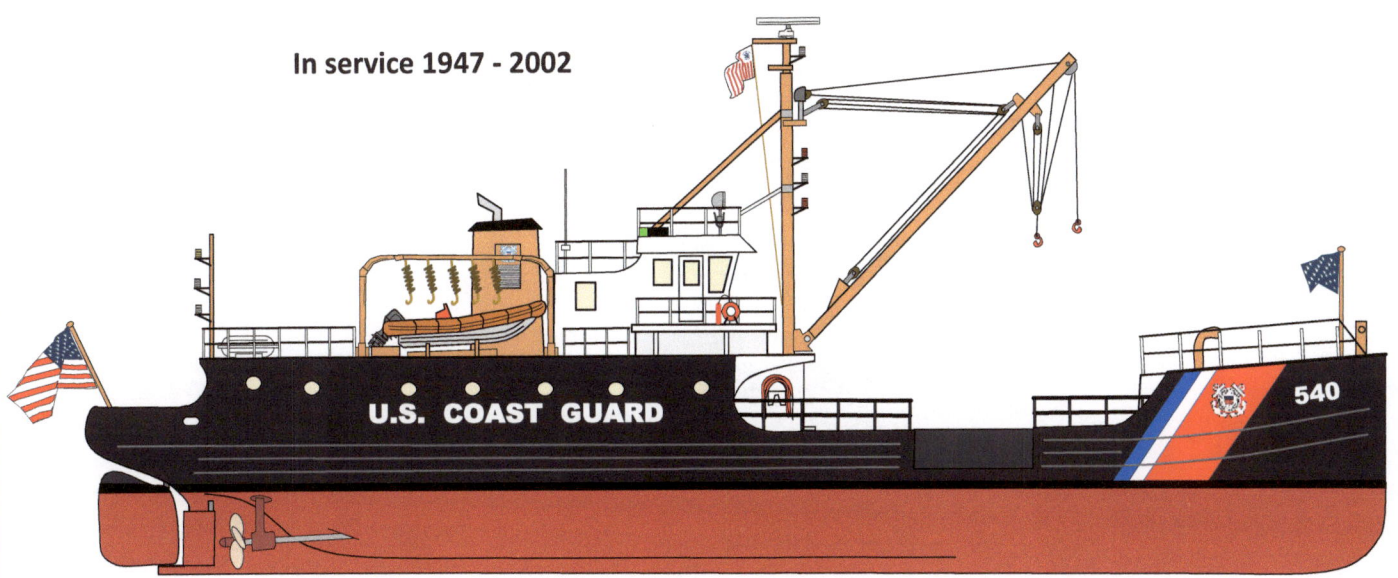

Displacement	600 tons
Length	132 ft 10 in Beam 30 ft 0 in Draft 8 ft 9 in
Installed power	2 × Union diesel engines 600 bhp
	2 × Caterpillar D-353-E diesel engine (1974
	2 × shafts 3 × rudders
Speed	10.5 knots
Range	2,450 nm at 10.5 knots 2,830 nmi at 7.5 knots
lifting capacity	20,000 pounds
Complement	26

157 FOOT RED CLASS BUOY TENDER (WLM)

Built by   Coast Guard Yard in Curtis Bay, Md
Cost   3.1 million each
Numbered   685 – 689
Built   5

In service 1964 - 1999

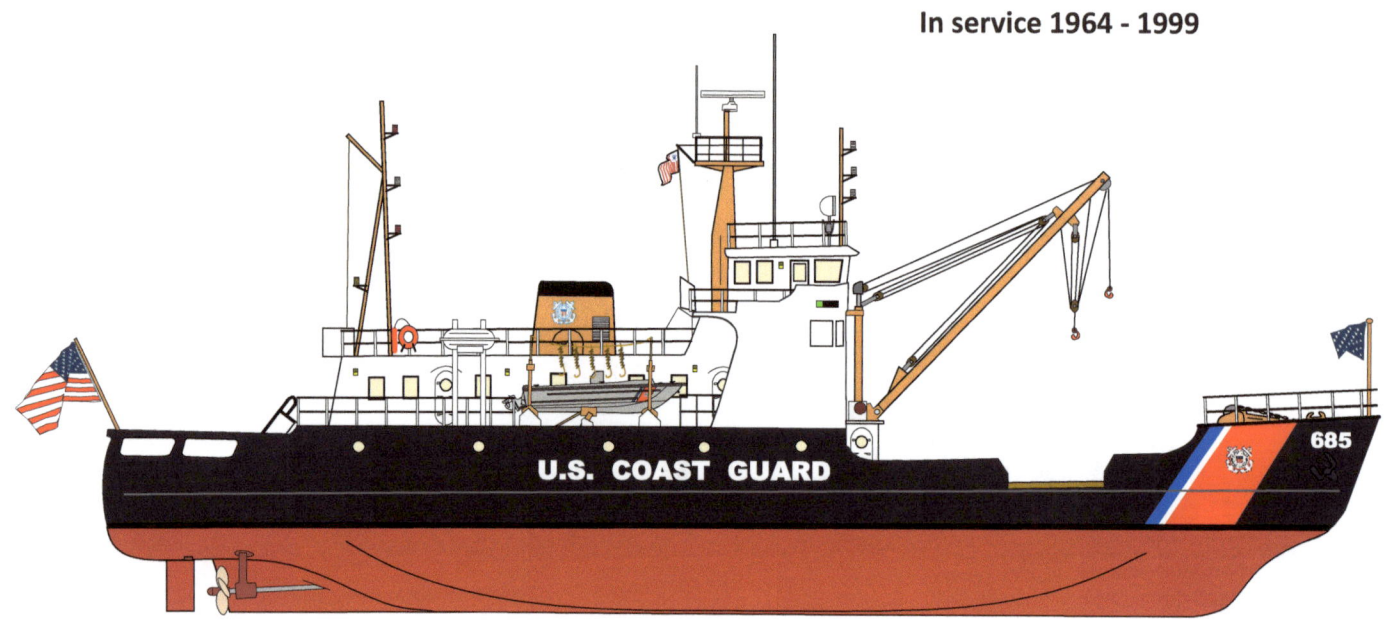

Displacement 572 t full load
Length 157 ft 10 in Beam 33 ft 0 in Draft 7 ft
Fuel   17,620 US gallons
Propulsion   2 × Caterpillar 398A Diesel engines 1,800 bhp
Speed 12.5 kn
Range 2,450 nmi at 10 kn
Complement   4 officers, 28 enlisted

175 FOOT HOLLYHOCK CLASS LIGHTHOUSE TENDER (WLM)

Builder Moore Dry Dock Company, Oakland, CA for the United States Lighthouse Service

Commissioned 1 October 1940 (USCG)

Cost $389,746

WLM 212 FIR

Queen of the fleet status 1988

In service 1937 - 1991

Displacement	885 tons.
Length	174 ft 8 in Beam 32 ft Draft 11 ft 3 in
Installed power	2 triple-expansion steam, horizontal engines 1,000 shp
	2 oil-fired Babcock & Wilcox watertube boilers
	Diesel conversion: (1951) 2 four-cylinder Fairbanks-Morse 38D 1,350 shp
	Detroit Diesel 100kW generators
	Propulsion Twin screws
Speed	12 knots
Range	2,000 mi
Complement	4 officers, 1 warrant officer, 69 enlisted (1945)
hoisting capacity	15 ton

Ice class Reinforced bow and stern. Ice-belt at water-line, notched forefoot.

175 FOOT KEEPER CLASS COASTAL BUOY TENDER (WLM)

Builders	Marinette Marine Corporation
Built	1995–1999
Completed	14
Cost total	$291 million 14 ships

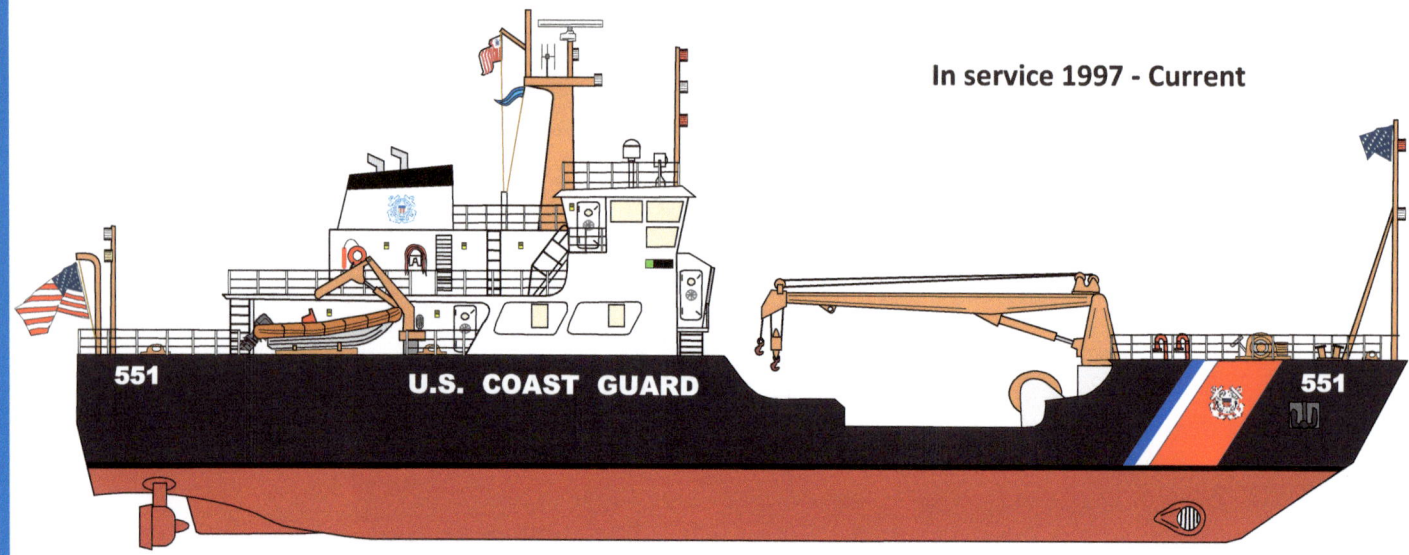

In service 1997 - Current

Displacement	850 long tons
Length	175 ft Beam 36 ft Draft 8 ft
Installed power	3 Caterpillar 3406 DITA generators which produce 285 kW each
Propulsion	2 Caterpillar 3508 DITA diesel engines 1,000 hp each bow thruster, 500 hp two Ulstein Z-drives
Fuel	16,385 US gallons
Speed	12 knots
Range	2,000 nmi at 10 knots
Complement	2 officers and 22 enlisted personnel
Crane capacity	20,000 pounds

Dynamic Positioning System
Capable of breaking flat 9-inch thick ice at 3 knots

180 FOOT SEAGOING BUOY TENDER (WLB)

Builders	Class A, B, C Zenith Dredge Company, Duluth, Mi Marine iron and shipbuilding, Duluth, MI Coast Guard yard Curtis bay Md 1942–1944	Class A (Cactus) Class B (Mesquite) Class C (Iris)	13 built $952,109 each 6 built $1,388,337 each 20 built $927,156 each
Number	62-407		
Total built	39		

In service 1942 - 2006

Typical specs		
	Displacement	1,025 tons
	Length	180 ft Beam 37 ft Draft 12 ft
	Propulsion	2 × General Motors EMD 645 V8 diesel engines
	Speed	8.3 knots cruising 13 knots maximum
	Range	8,000 nm at 13 knots
	Complement	3 officers, 2 warrant officers, 42 enlisted
	Armament	Wartime 1 × 3 in gun 20 mm guns Depth charges

225 FOOT JUNIPER CLASS SEAGOING BUOY TENDER (WLB)

Builder   Marinette Marine Corporation in Wi
                 16 Built between 1995 to 2004
Numbered 201 to 216

In service 1996 - Current

Displacement 2,000 tons (full load)
Length   225 ft Beam 46 ft Draft 13 ft
Propulsion   Two 3,100 hp Caterpillar diesel engines
Speed   16 knots
Range: 6,000 nautical miles at 12 knots
Complement   8 officers, 40 enlisted
Armament   Provision for 1 x Mk 38 25 mm naval gun
                  2 x .50 caliber machine guns

BUOY AND CONTRUCTION TENDER NAMES

225' Juniper Class Seagoing Buoy Tenders (WLB)

USCGC JUNIPER (WLB-201)
USCGC WILLOW (WLB-202)
USCGC KUKUI (WLB-203)
USCGC ELM (WLB-204)
USCGC WALNUT (WLB-205)
USCGC SPAR (WLB-206)
USCGC MAPLE (WLB-207)
USCGC ASPEN (WLB-208)
USCGC SYCAMORE (WLB-209)
USCGC CYPRESS (WLB-210)
USCGC OAK (WLB-211)
USCGC HICKORY (WLB-212)
USCGC FIR (WLB-213)
USCGC HOLLYHOCK (WLB-214)
USCGC SEQUOIA (WLB-215)
USCGC ALDER (WLB-216)

180' USCG Seagoing Buoy Tenders (WLB)

Class A (Cactus):

USCGC BALSAM (WLB-62)
USCGC CACTUS (WLB-270)
USCGC COWSLIP (WLB-277)
USCGC WOODBINE (WLB-289)
USCGC GENTIAN (WLB-290)
USCGC LAUREL (WLB-291)
USCGC CLOVER (WLB-292)
USCGC EVERGREEN (WLB-295)
USCGC SORREL (WLB-296)
USCGC CITRUS (WLB-300)
USCGC CONIFER (WLB-301)
USCGC MADRONA (WLB-302)
USCGC TUPELO (WLB-303)

Class B (Mesquite):

USCGC IRONWOOD (WLB-297)
USCGC MESQUITE (WLB-305)
USCGC BUTTONWOOD (WLB-306)
USCGC PLANETREE (WLB-307)
USCGC PAPAW (WLB-308)
USCGC SWEETGUM (WLB-309)

Class C (Iris):

USCGC BASSWOOD (WLB-388)
USCGC BITTERSWEET (WLB-389)
USCGC BLACKHAW (WLB-390)
USCGC BLACKTHORN (WLB-391)
USCGC BRAMBLE (WLB-392)
USCGC FIREBUSH (WLB-393)
USCGC HORNBEAM (WLB-394)
USCGC IRIS (WLB-395)
USCGC MALLOW (WLB-396)
USCGC MARIPOSA (WLB-397)
USCGC REDBUD (WLB-398)
USCGC SAGEBRUSH (WLB-399)
USCGC SALVIA (WLB-400)
USCGC SASSAFRAS (WLB-401)
USCGC SEDGE (WLB-402)
USCGC SPAR (WLB-403)
USCGC SUNDEW (WLB-404)
USCGC SWEETBRIER (WLB-405)
USCGC ACACIA (WLB-406)
USCGC WOODRUSH (WLB-407)

175' Buoy Tender Hollyhock Class (WLM)

USCGC FIR (WLM-212)
USCGC HOLLYHOCK (WLM-220)
USCGC WALNUT (WLM-252)

BUOY AND CONTRUCTION TENDER NAMES

175' Keeper Class Coastal Buoy Tender (WLM)
USCGC IDA LEWIS (WLM-551)
USCGC KATHERINE WALKER (WLM-552)
USCGC ABBIE BURGESS (WLM-553)
USCGC MARCUS HANNA (WLM-554)
USCGC JAMES RANKIN (WLM-555)
USCGC JOSHUA APPLEBY (WLM-556)
USCGC FRANK DREW (WLM-557)
USCGC ANTHONY PETIT (WLM-558)
USCGC BARBARA MABRITY (WLM-559)
USCGC WILLIAM TATE (WLM-560)
USCGC HARRY CLAIBORNE (WLM-561)
USCGC MARIA BRAY (WLM-562)
USCGC HENRY BLAKE (WLM-563)
USCGC GEORGE COBB (WLM-564)

160' Inland Construction Tender (WLIC)
USCGC PAMLICO (WLIC-800)
USCGC HUDSON (WLIC-801)
USCGC KENNEBEC (WLIC-802)
USCGC SAGINAW (WLIC-803)

157' Red Class Coastal Buoy Tender (WLM)
USCGC RED WOOD (WLM-685)
USCGC RED BEECH (WLM-686)
USCGC RED BIRCH (WLM-687)
USCGC RED CEDAR (WLM-688)
USCGC RED OAK (WLM-689)

133' White Class Coastal Buoy Tender (WAGL/WLM)
USCGC WHITE SUMAC (WLM-540)
USCGC WHITE ALDER (WLM-541)
USCGC WHITE BUSH (WLM-542)
USCGC WHITE HOLLY (WLM-543)
USCGC WHITE SAGE (WLM-544)
USCGC WHITE HEATH (WLM-545)
USCGC WHITE LUPINE (WLM-546)
USCGC WHITE PINE (WLM-547)

100' Inland Buoy Tender (WLI)
USCGC BLUEBELL (WLI-313)
USCGC BUCKTHORN (WLI-642)

128' lightship (WLV)
USCGC NANTUCKET I (WLV-612)
USCGC NANTUCKET II (WLV-613)

100' Inland Construction Tender (WLIC)
USCGC SMILAX (WLIC-315)

80' Inland Buoy Tender (WLI)
USCGC TERN (WLI-80801)

75' Gasconade Class River Buoy Tender (WLR)
USCGC GASCONADE (WLR-75401)
USCGC MUSKINGUM (WLR-75402)
USCGC WYACONDA (WLR-75403)
USCGC CHIPPEWA (WLR-75404)
USCGC CHEYENNE (WLR-75405)
USCGC KICKAPOO (WLR-75406)
USCGC KANAWHA (WLR-75407)
USCGC PATOKA (WLR-75408)
USCGC CHENA (WLR-75409)

75' Kankakee Class River Buoy Tender (WLR)
USCGC KANKAKEE (WLR-75500)
USCGC GREENBRIER (WLR-75501)

BUOY AND CONTRUCTION TENDER NAMES

75' Inland Construction Tender (WLIC)

USCGC ANVIL (WLIC-75301)

USCGC HAMMER (WLIC-75302)

USCGC SLEDGE (WLIC-75303)

USCGC MALLET (WLIC-75304)

USCGC VISE (WLIC-75305)

USCGC CLAMP (WLIC-75306)

USCGC WEDGE (WLIC-75307)

USCGC SPIKE (WLIC-75308)

USCGC HATCHET (WLIC-75309)

USCGC AXE (WLIC-75310)

65' River Buoy Tender (WLR)

USCGC OUACHITA (WLR-65501)

USCGC CIMARRON (WLR-65502)

USCGC OBION (WLR-65503)

USCGC SCIOTO (WLR-65504)

USCGC OSAGE (WLR-65505)

USCGC SANGAMON (WLR-65506)

65' Inland Buoy Tender (WLI)

USCGC BAYBERRY (WLI-65400)

USCGC ELDERBERRY (WLI-65401)

USCGC BLUEBERRY (WLI-65402)

USCGC BLACKBERRY (WLI-65303)

USCGC CHOKEBERRY (WLI-65304)

USCGC LOGANBERRY (WLI-65305)

Helicopters

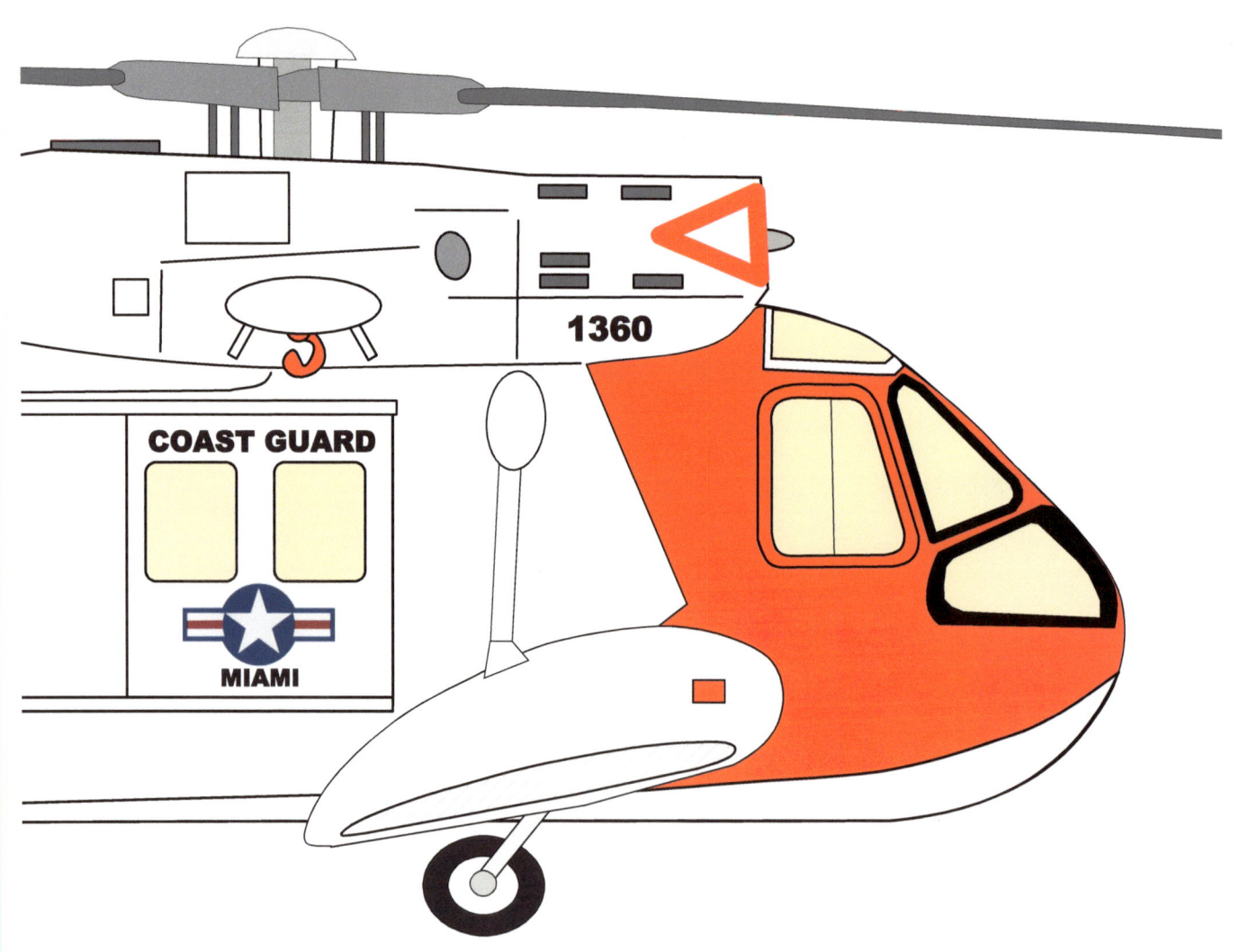

HH 52A	**Search and Rescue - utility helicopter**
HH 3F	**Medium-lift transport - Search and Rescue helicopter**
HH 60J/T	**Medium-range recovery helicopter**
MH 65C	**Short Range Search and rescue helicopter**

With the exception of the HH 3F Pelican, all other helicopters could be deployed onboard cutters or Icebreakers for search and rescue or law enforcement operations. Onboard icebreakers are used to seek out a favorable route through the ice. The HH 52A Seaguard and the HH 3F Pelican were also amphibious and had the ability to land on water to recover survivors.

MH 68A	**Short Range Armed Interdiction helicopter**
MH 90	**Short Range Armed Interdiction helicopter**

Both the MH 68A Stingray and the MH 90 Enforcer were assigned to the Helicopter Interdiction Tactical Squadron (HITRON). This was an armed Coast Guard helicopter squadron specializing in airborne use of force and drug-interdiction missions. The Enforcer was used for proof of concept and the Stingray was put into service afterwards. Both were deployed onboard cutters for drug interdiction and law enforcement patrols. During the early stages, HITRIN and the armed helicopter's existence was a classified operation.

HH-52A SEAGUARD

Manufacturer Sikorsky Aircraft Corporation   Aircraft Type   SAR/utility amphibious Helicopter
Designation   HH-52A
Number built 99
Cost $250,000 (1963)

In service 1961 - 1989

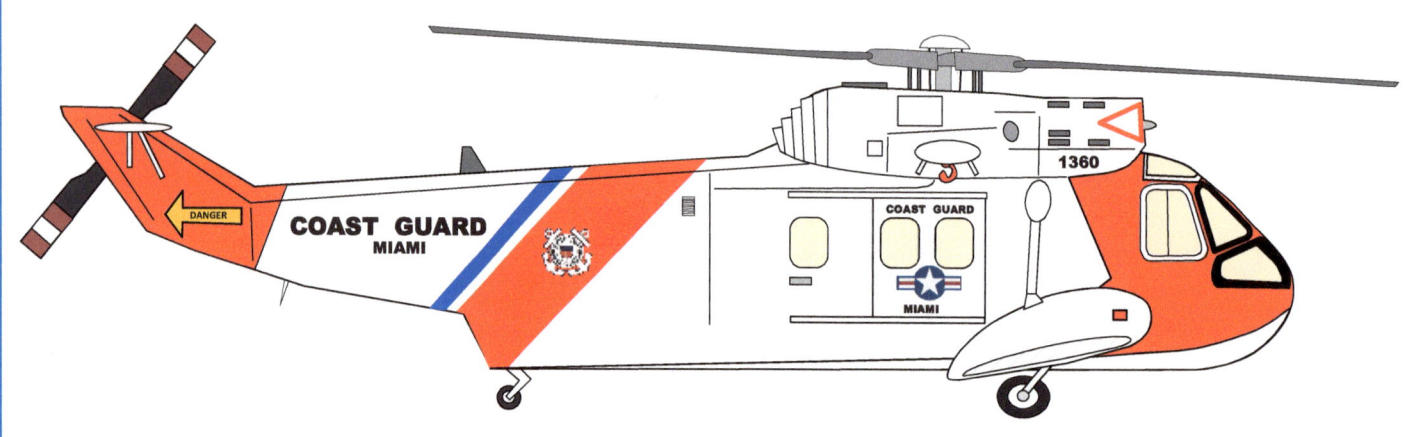

Gross Weight:	8,300 lb. Empty Weight: 5,083 lb.
Rotor Diameter:	53 ft 0 in. Blade Area: 2,206 sq. ft.
Height:	16 ft. 0 in. Length: 44 ft. 6.5 in.
Top Speed:	109 kts. Cruising Speed: 85 kts.
Sea Level Climb:	1,080 ft./min.
Range:	474 nm.
GService Ceiling:	11,200 ft.
Powerplant:	General Electric T-58-GE-8B turboshaft (1,250 shp. Derated to 730 shp.
Takeoff Power:	730 shp.
Crew:	3
Passengers	10

HH-52A SEAGUARD

Manufacturer Sikorsky Aircraft Corporation
Designation HH-52A
Aircraft Type Amphibious Helicopter
Cost $250,000 (1963)

Aircraft Type   SAR/utility amphibious Helicopter

Designation: S-62C, HU2S-1G

In service 1961 - 1989

POLAR OPERATIONS DIVISION (POPDIV)

Carried onboard Wind, Glacier, and Polar icebreakers. Painted red to contrast against the snow and ice.

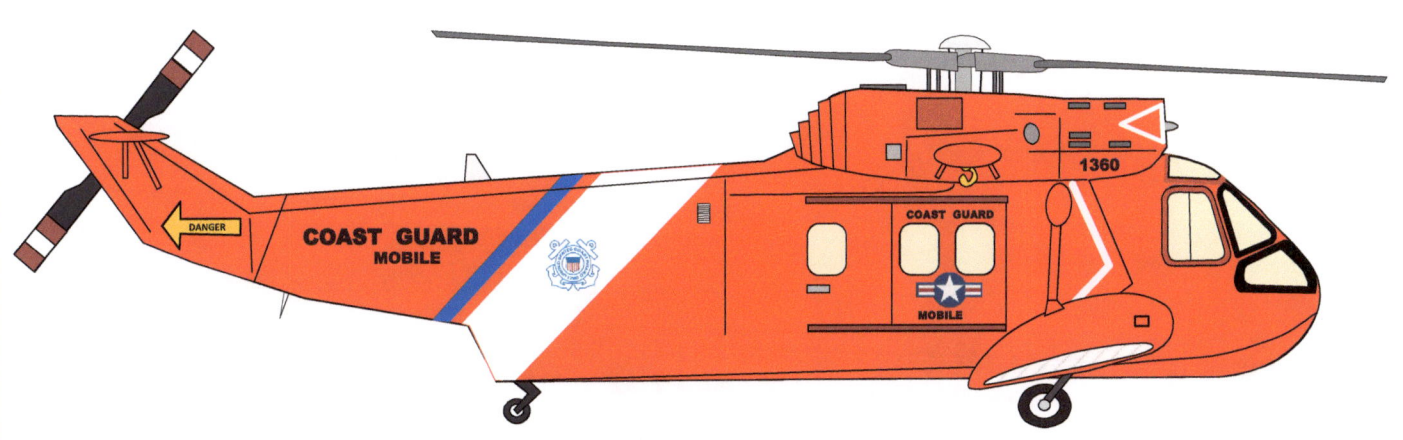

Gross Weight:	8,300 lb. Empty Weight: 5,083 lb.
Rotor Diameter:	53 ft 0 in. Blade Area: 2,206 sq. ft.
Height:	16 ft. 0 in. Length: 44 ft. 6.5 in.
Top Speed:	109 kts. Cruising Speed: 85 kts.
Sea Level	Climb:1,080 ft./min.
Range:	474 nm.
GService Ceiling:	11,200 ft.
Powerplant:	General Electric T-58-GE-8B turboshaft (1,250 shp. Derated to 730 shp.
Takeoff Power:	730 shp.
Crew:	3
Passengers	10

HH3F PELICAN

Manufacturer	Sikorsky Agusta
First flight	1959
Units Built for Coast Guard	40

In service 1967 - 1994

Aircraft Type   twin turbine, medium range, amphibious, all weather helicopter

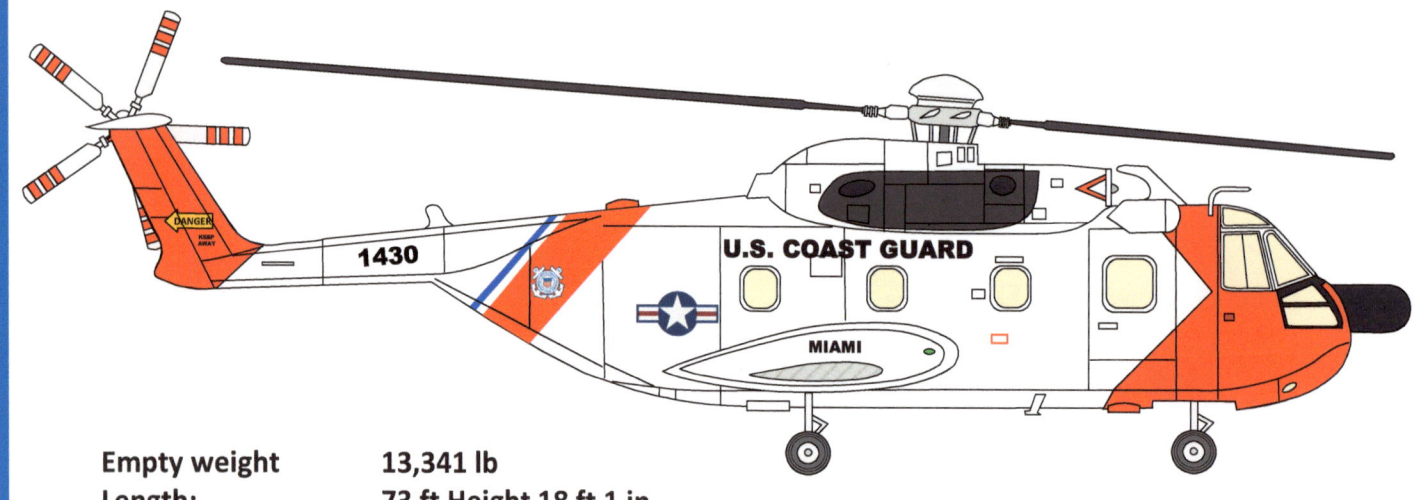

Empty weight	13,341 lb
Length:	73 ft Height 18 ft 1 in
Max takeoff weight	22,050 lb
Main rotor diameter	62 ft
Main rotor area	3,019 sq ft 5-bladed main rotor
Powerplant:	2 × General Electric T58-GE-10 turboshaft engines, 1,400 shp each
Fuel capacity:	683 US gal
Maximum speed	143 knots
Service ceiling	21,000 ft IGE
Rate of climb	2,220 ft/min
Range	779 nm
Crew	3
Capacity	28 pax

HH-60J/60T JAYHAWK

Manufacturer	Sikorsky Aircraft	Aircraft type	Multi-mission, twin-engine, medium-range helicopter
First flight	8 August 1989		
Produced	1990–1996		
Number built	42 (+ 3 conversions)	Designated HH-60J before being upgraded and redesignated beginning in 2007	

In service 1990 - Current

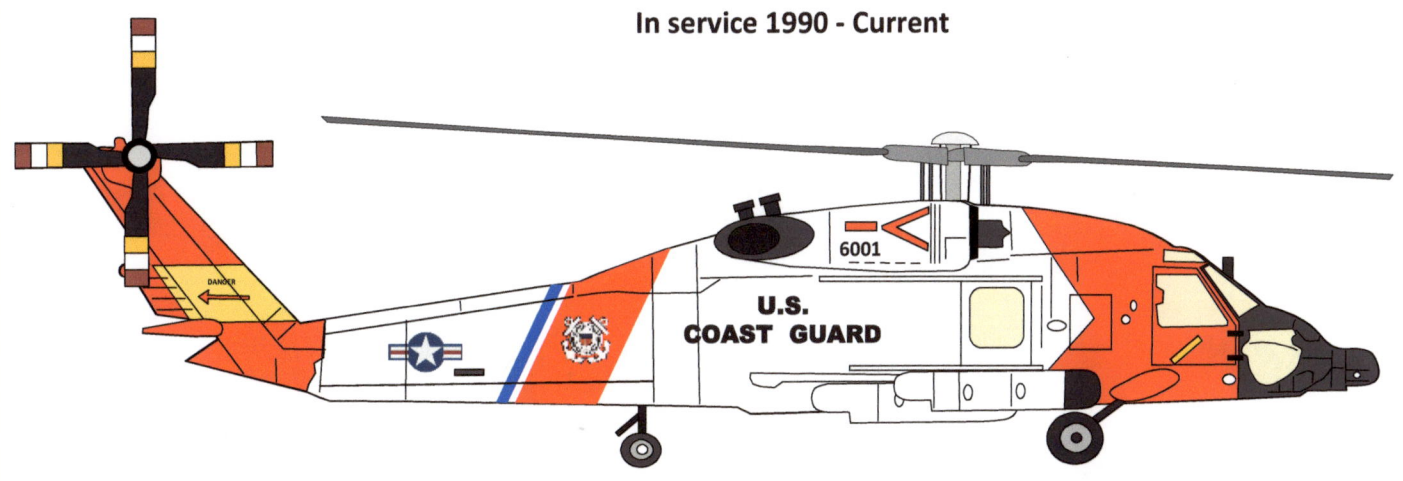

Empty weight	14,500 lb Max takeoff weight 21,884 lb
Length	64 ft 10 in Wingspan 53 ft 8 in Height 17 ft 0 in
Powerplant	2 × General Electric T700-GE-401C gas turbines, 1,890 shp each
Performance	Maximum speed: 205 mph Cruise speed: 160 mph
Range	802 mi
Service ceiling	5,000 ft hovering
Crew	four (pilot, co-pilot, two flight crew)
Armament	1 × 0.308 in M240H medium machine gun in starboard door
	1 × 0.50 in Barrett M82 semi-automatic rifle

HH-60J/60T JAYHAWK

Manufacturer	Sikorsky Aircraft
First flight	8 August 1989
Produced	1990–1996
Number built	42 (+ 3 convrsions)

CENTENNIAL AIRCRAFT

The Jayhawk helicopter is painted yellow to represent the chrome yellow paint scheme that US Coast Guard and US Navy helicopters used in the late 1940s and early 1950s. Examples include the Sikorsky HO3S-1G and the Sikorsky HO4S.

Altogether, 16 Coast Guard aircraft received historic paint schemes representing various eras of Coast Guard aviation, including Jayhawk and Dolphin helicopters, as well as HC-144 Ocean Sentry fixed-wing aircraft.

US Coast Guard aviation officially began on 1 April 1916 when 3rd Lt Elmer Stone reported to flight training in Pensacola, Florida. The Coast Guard celebrated 100 years of Coast Guard aviation throughout 2016.

MH-65C DOLPHIN

Manufacturer	Aérospatiale Helicopter Corporation
	American Eurocopter
First flight	1980
Number built	102
Aircraft Type	Short range search and rescue and recovery aircraft

In service 1985 - Current

Length	38 ft 1 in Height: 13 ft 1 in
Empty weight	6,896 lb Max takeoff weight: 9,480 lb
Powerplant	2 × Turbomeca Arriel 2C2-CG turboshaft engines, 853 hp each
Main rotor diameter	39 ft 1 in Main rotor area: 1,197.2 sq ft
Performance	Maximum speed: 210 mph Cruise speed 150 mph
Range	355 nm
Service ceiling	17,999 ft
Crew	2 pilots and 2 crew
Armament Guns:	1 x 7.62 mm M240 machine gun
	1 x Barrett M107 0.50 in (12.70 mm) caliber precision rifle

MH-65C DOLPHIN

Manufacturer	Aérospatiale Helicopter Corporation
	American Eurocopter
First flight	1980
Number built	102

CENTENNIAL AIRCRAFT

Altogether, 16 Coast Guard aircraft received historic paint schemes representing various eras of Coast Guard aviation, including Jayhawk and Dolphin helicopters, as well as HC-144 Ocean Sentry fixed-wing aircraft.

US Coast Guard aviation officially began on 1 April 1916 when 3rd Lt Elmer Stone reported to flight training in Pensacola, Florida. The Coast Guard celebrated 100 years of Coast Guard aviation throughout 2016.

MH-90 ENFORCER

Manufacturer	McDonnell Douglas Helicopter Systems MD Helicopters
Aircraft type	short-range armed interdiction helicopter
	Attached to the Helicopter Interdiction Tactical Squadron (HITRON)

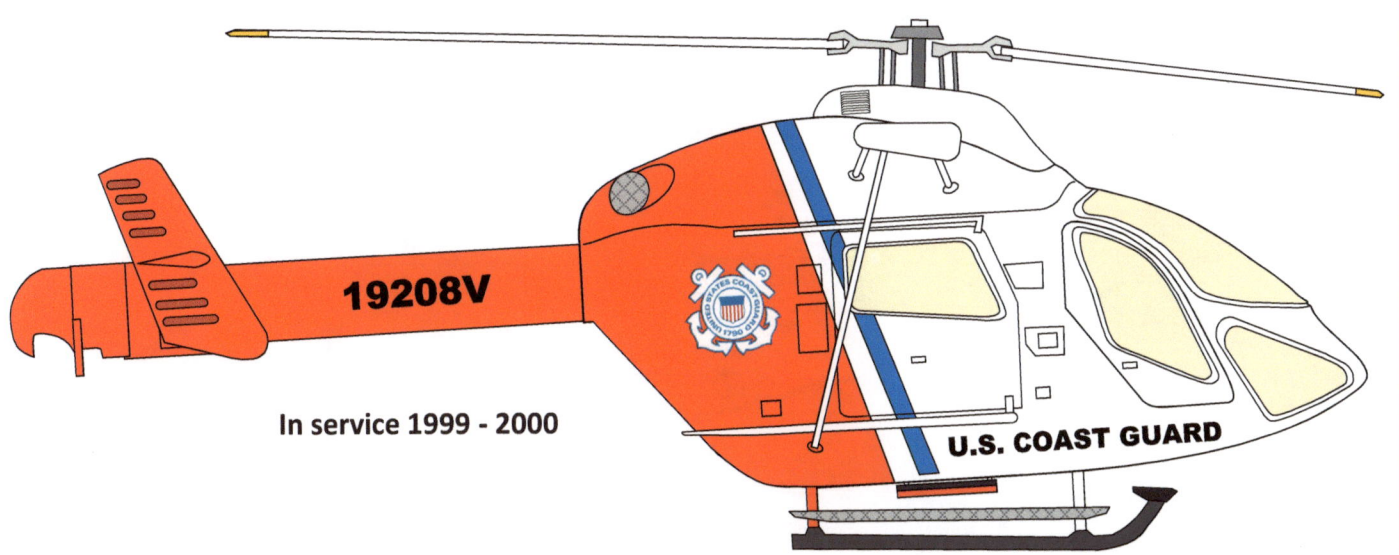

In service 1999 - 2000

Max takeoff weight:	6,250 lb
Length:	32 ft 4 in Height: 12 ft 0 in
Main rotor diameter:	33 ft 10 in
Main rotor area:	899.16 sq ft
Performance	Cruise speed: 154 mph at sea level
Never exceed speed:	160 mph
Range:	293 nm
Service ceiling:	17,500 ft
Hover ceiling IGE:	11,000 ft at International Standard Atmosphere
Rate of climb:	1,000 ft/min
Powerplant:	2 × Pratt & Whitney Canada PW206E turboshaft engines, 550 shp each
Crew:	3
Capacity:	3,000 lb slung load

MH-68A STINGRAY

Manufacturer	Augusta
	Agusta Westland
	Leonardo S.p.A.
Built	8

In service 2000 - 2008

Aircraft type   short-range armed interdiction helicopter

Attached to the Helicopter Interdiction Tactical Squadron (HITRON)

Empty weight	3,505 lb
Max takeoff weight	6,283 lb
Length	37 ft 7 in Height: 11 ft 6 in
Main rotor diameter	36 ft 1 in
Powerplant	2 × Pratt & Whitney Canada PW206C Turboshaft engine 560 hp each
Performance	Maximum speed 168 knots, Cruise speed 154 knots
Never exceed speed	168 knots
Rate of climb	1,930 ft/min
Crew	3
Weapons	M-16 5.56mm rifles and M240 7.62mm machine guns
	RC50 laser-sighted .50 caliber precision rifle

Almost immediately following the attacks on 11 September 2001, all bridges and tunnels in Manhattan were closed, leaving hundreds of thousands of people stranded with no way to return safely home. Coast Guard personnel, taking charge of the situation, directed the safe evacuation of more than 500,000 people off the island using hundreds of local ferries, and commercial and private craft. This, the largest maritime evacuation in recorded history, was conducted in less than 8 hours, with no loss of life.

In support of Operation Noble Eagle, thousands of Coast Guard men and women Reservists and Auxiliarists were mobilized to support the largest homeland defense and port security operations since World War II, ensuring the safety of maritime commerce, continued operation of port facilities, search and rescue and other vital operations.

COMMANDING OFFICERS, COXSWAINS, AND CUTTER CREW INSIGNIAS

COMMAND AFLOAT

Commissioned and warrant officers wear this badge when they are the commanding officer or Captain of the cutter.

BOATSWAINS MATE

The enlisted Boatswains mate rating is the only rating that can command cutters and small boats.

OFFICER IN CHARGE AFLOAT

Petty officers and chief petty officers wear this badge when they are the Officer in charge or Captain of the cutter.

CUTTERMAN INSIGNIA OFFICER

Pin is awarded on a temporary basis after six months of sea time. The award becomes permanent after 5 years of cumulative sea time in the Coast Guard.

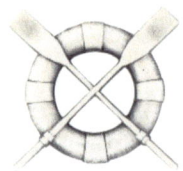

SURFMAN BADGE

Enlisted personnel or officers who are qualified as Coxswains and are authorized to operate surf boats in heavy surf, extreme weather, and sea conditions.

CUTTERMAN INSIGNIA ENLISTED

Pin is awarded on a temporary basis after six months of sea time. The award becomes permanent after 5 years of cumulative sea time in the Coast Guard.

COXSWAINS INSIGNIA

Enlisted personnel in charge of a small boat are a coxswain or captain of the vessel. They are the senior person onboard while underway regardless of rank or seniority.

ENLISTED RANKS

SEAMAN RECRUIT		PETTY OFFICER 3RD CLASS		
SEAMAN APPRENTICE		PETTY OFFICER 2ND CLASS	 	
SEAMAN		PETTY OFFICER 1ST CLASS	 	
FIREMAN APPRENTICE				

CHIEF PETTY OFFICER	 		
SENIOR CHIEF PETTY OFFICER	 		
MASTER CHIEF PETTY OFFICER	 		
MASTER CHIEF PETTY OFFICER OF THE COAST GUARD	 		

FIREMAN

AIRMAN APPRENTICE

AIRMAN

WARRANT OFFICER RANKS

Chief warrant officer 2

Chief warrant officer 3

Chief warrant officer 4

U.S. Coast Guard Chief Warrant Officer specialty markings (collar)

Aviation Engineering (AVI)

Bandmaster (BNDM) | Boatswain (BOSN) | Diving Specialist (DIV) | Electronics (ELC) | Investigator (INV)

Intelligence System Specialist (ISS) | Marine Safety Specialist Deck (MSSD) | Marine Safety Specialist Engineer (MSSE) | Marine Safety Specialist Response (MSSR) | Finance & Supply (F&S)

Material Maintenance (MAT) | Information Systems Management (ISM) | Medical Administration (MED) | Naval Engineering (ENG) | Maritime Law Enforcement Specialist (MLES)

Personnel Administration (PERS) | Port Safety & Security (PSS) | Public Information (INF) | Weapons (WEPS) | Operations Systems Specialist (OSS)

OFFICER RANKS

ENSIGN

Lieutenant (junior grade)

Lieutenant

Lieutenant commander

Commander

CAPTAIN

Rear admiral (Lower Half)

Rear admiral (Upper Half)

Vice admiral

Admiral

About the Author

Running the Duane's 26 ft. MSB somewhere in the western north Atlantic, 1984

Doug has spent his life going to sea. It started at the age of 16 attending Naval boot camp with the U.S. Naval Sea Cadets, and closely followed up with joining the Coast Guard, all before the age of 20. Serving onboard the WHEC Duane out of Portland ME in the early 80's was followed by training at Yorktown BM "A" school. As a newly promoted 3rd class boatswain's mate, Doug was transferred to district 7 and conducted search and rescue and law enforcement operations in the Miami area. This was at the height of the drug war and just after the Mariel boatlift, hectic to say the least. At the age of 26 Doug Moved into the private sector and immediately took command of a 106 ft. yacht that cruised globally.

Over the past 30 years Doug has run some very popular and high-profile mega yachts Doug was honored by winning five Antiqua Charter Yacht Show awards and four Boat International/US Classic Yacht awards. His latest awards include the 2017 Newport charter show for Best Charter Crew at the "Charter Yacht Hop Event" and the 2019 Newport charter show for Best Charter Crew. Doug is well known in yachting circles and has spent the last 13 years on his current command, the Motor Yacht Renaissance, starting as build captain.

www.ingramcontent.com/pod-product-compliance
Lightning Source LLC
Chambersburg PA
CBHW041520220426
43667CB00003B/54